my style, my place

» by Allyce King and Nicole Thieret

©2007 by Allyce King and Nicole Thieret

Published by

kp **krause publications**
An Imprint of F+W Publications

700 East State Street • Iola, WI 54990-0001
715-445-2214 • 888-457-2873
www.krausebooks.com

Our toll-free number to place an order or obtain a free catalog is (800) 258-0929.

The following trademarked terms and companies appear in this publication:

Armani, Bernina, Big Pony Polo, Dolce and Gabbana, Dritz© Fray Check™, Horchow, iPod™, Louis Vuitton, Pottery Barn, Starbucks, Velcro™, Williams Sonoma, X-acto™

Library of Congress Control Number: 2007928419

ISBN-13: 978-0-89689-538-6
ISBN-10: 0-89689-538-6

Photography by Lance Tilford

Designed by Katrina Newby

Edited by Erica Swanson

Printed in China

acknowledgments

From Allyce: I would like to thank my mother, Cindy Cummins, who truly made this book what it is today. Thank you for your dedication, inspiration, motivation, editing and late-night sewing. I would like to say thanks to my grandparents, Carol and Ronald Faupel, for all the support, for believing in us, and for letting me turn their basement into a sewing sweatshop on the weekends. A special thanks to Mr. and Mrs. Thieret, who offered a home-away-from-home while Nicole and I worked last summer. To Nicole, my friend and co-author: fate has really led us to where we are today. We have had so much in common, from pageants to fashion to hobbies. Our friendship is one-of-a-kind. Thanks for the all-night slumber parties in the sewing room and the never-ending fashion gossip.

From Nicole: I want to start by saying thanks to my parents. Without you, none of this would have been possible. You helped me financially (my personal bank account) and emotionally (my psychiatrists). You offered up your basement for an entire summer and never said a word about the constant mess (though I know you thought it). And another thanks to you, Mom, for helping me on two of the projects. To Cindy, who is now like my second mom, none of this would have happened if it weren't for you and all your help. You truly are an amazing person, and I feel so privileged to be working next to you. To Allyce, my partner in crime, it really was fate that night we met at the pageant in Poplar Bluff. You're my favorite stay-up-late, eat-out-all-the-time, complain-about-school and gossip buddy, not to mention my favorite roommate! And to all the other people who have been there to help me through the ups and downs during the creation of this book: all of your support is much appreciated!

From both of us: We would like to start by saying thanks to Lance Tilford and Tamara Tungate for all their hard work and expertise, resulting in spectacular photos; you both helped to capture the spirit and energy of this project. A special thanks goes to our models, Ashley Green, Sarah Cecchettini, Monet Stunson and Brian Schwarze, for your dedication. The pictures wouldn't have been great without you. Thanks to Mary Mikret for all your support and help in the beginning of this journey. You truly were an inspiration. Thanks to Jeanne Delpit at Bernina of America for all your help and persistence, and to Pam Hastings for the wonderful projects you helped us finish. And to Stephanie Link, thanks so much for the wonderful illustrations that helped to shape the book into what it is.

Contents

M Y P L A C E

introduction

It was the party of the century, and everyone who was anyone was going! Well, maybe that's a bit of an exaggeration. When I say party of the century, I mean more like the month. And when I say everyone who was anyone, I mean just the unbelievably well-dressed people. You know who they are — they wear Dolce & Gabbana sunglasses and carry Louis Vuitton purses. Even the guys were wearing Big Pony Polos or something great from Armani.

So here was our dilemma: if everyone invited was unbelievably wealthy enough to afford designer clothes, what the heck were we going to wear? This is an age-old problem for most women, and it's even worse when you have a closet full of clothes. But let's be serious here, there was no way that we could come up with a great designer outfit in a week. We had nice outfits, but we were well-dressed on a normal college student level. So, how could we wear affordable clothes and not stick out like Skreech Powers at a debutante ball? The answer was simple — we decided to re-design something from our own closets.

We started looking online and through all of our magazines in search of the perfect outfit. We wanted something no one would have, but we also didn't want over-the-top haute couture. Whatever it was, it had to be easy; between projects at school and work, we had very little time to get these outfits together. Finally, we came up with a plan. After ransacking our closets, we found clothes that we could bear to cut up, and we changed them into something else. With a little bit of ingenuity and creativity, we created great ready-to-wear pieces straight from the runway.

We were a hit! Everyone loved our take on the new looks for the season, even if they had no clue which designers were our inspiration. The best part was that we definitely fit in with all the people in swanky clothes. As we walked around the apartment, we started to see fashion in another sense: home interior. The apartment was immaculate! There were things from Pottery Barn, William Sonoma and even Horchow — we're talking big bucks here — and it was all to die for. Now we had a new idea: if we could recreate designer outfits, why couldn't we recreate designer home fashions?

Even though we didn't have an apartment, we did have suite-style dorm rooms (our own room with a shared bathroom). We may not have been able to use all of the home fashions we liked, but we could use some of them. Now, if any of our new friends wanted to come visit our dorms, we could invite them in comfortably! The entire party was a smash hit; we came out with great outfits and a new smashing dorm room! Now when people see our rooms and clothes, they all say the same thing: "You are such creative girls."

We know you want easy-to-create projects that don't look like things your 12-year-old sister made in home ec. The designs in this book are quick do-it-yourself designs that will be useful and not tacky, a great combination. With a mixture of clothing fashions and home fashions, you'll find great projects to fit your needs. All you need is a little creativity!

Chapter 1

getting started

We know it can be intimidating when you first start sewing. But don't worry—that's what we're here for! You will pick things up along the way that will make the sewing process go faster.

If you're afraid that it will take you years to learn the little tricks the pros use — forget about it! We are going to give you a few tips to make you feel like you've been sewing for months. Start with these techniques:

- When threading your sewing machine, begin by putting your presser foot down. This will make it a lot easier to see what you are doing.
- Set your machine on the lowest speed when you're first learning to sew. Get a feel for your machine, and increase the speed as you feel more comfortable.
- When sewing, keep your fingers far from the needle. Stop sewing and move your hand away from the needle when the fabric is getting close.
- Clip your threads as you go along. This will keep the threads from getting tangled and bunching.
- Be sure that you double-check measurements before cutting your fabric. You don't want to make an emergency run to the fabric store because you cut something too short and don't have enough fabric left to re-cut.
- Use pinking shears to finish the raw edges of fabric that can't be zigzag stitched, such as silk.
- Try using a safety pin to turn tubes right-side out. Start by pinning the safety pin in one end and pushing it through to the other end. When it's finished, it will be right-side out.
- When using an embroidery machine, keep a close eye on your needle. Switch to a new embroidery needle after every three or four designs, depending on the intricacy of the design, or the needle will become dull and break. You don't want to have to re-do an entire design!

Sewing should not be scary or frustrating. By taking your time and keeping a good sense of humor, sewing will be one of the most relaxing things you do. Just remember to have fun!

Finding Materials

To start your re-designed projects, go though your closets. Find articles of clothing that you don't wear anymore. Whether they are too small or are just outdated, chances are they can work to your benefit when redesigning. With a little ingenuity, you can use that old T-shirt to create a great new style. Everything in this book was made from clothes that we used to own. We took hot new designs from the runway and recreated them for us. Now you can do the same with your wardrobe!

If you can't find anything in your closet that you need for one of our projects, don't worry. Thrift stores might have what you are looking for. Now, I know what you're thinking — you wouldn't be caught dead in something from a thrift store. We used to feel the same way, until a project for one of Allyce's classes took her through a thrift store. After seeing all the retro vintage items, her opinion changed. How else do you think designers get inspiration for their vintage pieces? Of course their articles of clothing are made from scratch, but that's also why they are so expensive. Thrift stores can become your new best friend. Out of all the places we went shopping, thrift stores were our favorite. You can be inspired and have a lot of fun checking out old looks you thought had been buried with New Kids on the Block cassette tapes.

You can also look for cheap clothing in second-hand stores. Some people think of these as thrift stores, but thrift stores are a bit cheaper and usually have more dated clothing. Second-hand stores usually have great discounted prices for looks from one or two years ago. These stores usually get better name-brand clothes that you might find in a mall. Second-hand stores are great for those of you who still might have a hard time stepping into a thrift store — but you will pay a little extra for the things you buy.

Another great place to look for clothes is on the clearance racks in your favorite stores. You never know what you will find. Go with a friend, and turn the shopping trip into a scavenger hunt: whoever finds the best deal on a wearable item wins! If you find something that just isn't right, think of all the things you can do to make it wearable. Your local mall is a really great place to look for clothes, especially when all of last season's items are on sale. If you set a goal to not spend more than ten dollars on any one article of clothing, you are sure to stay under budget. Just remember not to buy anything you "may wear later" or "may use later," because nine times out of ten, you'll never use it for anything.

Choosing Fabric

Shopping for home interior items is a little more difficult than looking for clothing because you will need to find fabrics to use. If you have never purchased fabric before, this can be very intimidating. But don't worry — that's why you have us! When you go through the project supply lists, you will see that we have listed the fabric we used in the project. Just go into any local fabric store, and they can help you find the fabric or something comparable.

If you don't like our fabric choices, spend some time looking around. Let the fabric pick you. You will probably be drawn to a few key items. Pick them out, and find coordinating fabrics to go with them. If you want, you can use our projects as the centerpiece for designing your room. If you need help picking out color combinations, an associate at your local fabric store will be more than willing to help you find something to go with your choices.

Sewing Machines

If you don't have a sewing machine or embroidery machine, visit a local dealership. While you're there, you might want to sit down and learn a little about the machine. You can also look around at all of the machines they have to offer. Try them out, and go with the one you feel most comfortable using. The projects in the book can be made without using the embroidery designs, but if you have access to an embroidery machine, go for it!

Basic Supplies

Now you're all set! Start gathering the tools and materials you will need, and get started! To begin, you will need these supplies:

- Tape measure
- Fray check
- Marking chalk
- Straight pins
- Seam gauge
- Extra bobbins (see each project for specifications)
- Thread (see each project for specifications)
- Seam ripper
- Extra needles (machine, hand, embroidery, jean, etc.)
- Iron
- Pressing arm
- Shears (small trimming scissors, large fabric scissors and pinking shears)
- Fabric (see each project for specifications)
- Buttons (see each project for specifications)
- Trims (see each project for specifications)
- Sewing machine
- Embroidery machine (optional)
- Rotary cutter and mat
- Safety pins

Try using an embroidery machine to embellish home décor projects.

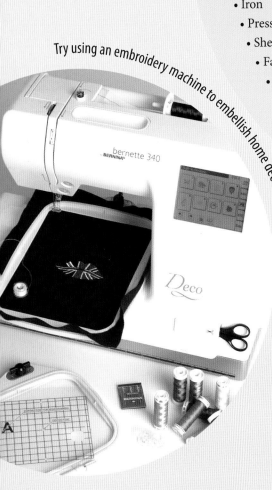

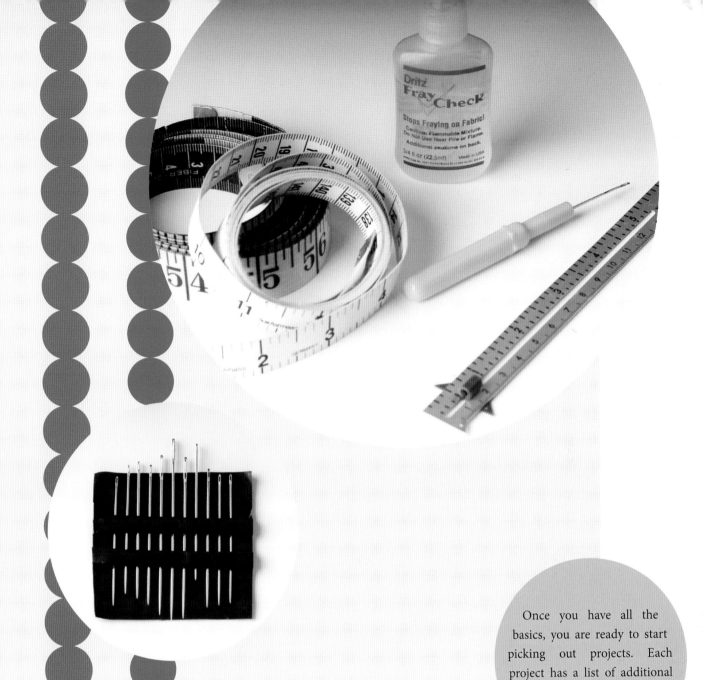

Once you have all the basics, you are ready to start picking out projects. Each project has a list of additional supplies that you will need as well.

A Few Guidelines

Before you begin a project, there are some basic guidelines you need to follow:
- All fashion clothing seams should be ⅝".
- All home décor seams should be ½".
- After sewing any kind of a seam, always press with an iron.
- Be careful not to sew through extra layers of fabric (i.e. don't sew the front of a shirt to the back).
- Take out straight pins as you get to them so you don't sew over them and break a needle.
- Double-check all measurements before you start sewing on a project. Everything needs to fit perfectly when pinned.

gotcha covered
— Activewear and Outerwear —

It was a Saturday morning in early fall, and the parking lot was full of students ready for the big game: Missouri vs. Kansas. The sun was shining down, and the air was still cool and crisp from the night before. It was the perfect setting for a great morning of tailgating.

We don't go to Mizzou, but we were spending a Saturday morning rooting for their victory over KU. Why? We go to an all-girl's school. We go to football games for one reason, and one reason only: to look at muscular guys in tight pants.

It was 9:30 in the morning, and everyone was getting pumped up. All of a sudden, a group of Mizzou guys playing football accidentally knocked over a barbeque grill belonging to guys from KU. To be nice, I offered to help before a fight broke loose (and hey, the KU guys were pretty hot). As I bent over to pick up the lid from the grill, I felt a breezy gust of air. Face flushing with embarrassment, I turned around to check — and yes, I definitely tore a hole in the seat of my jeans. There was no cartoonish ripping sound like you hear in the movies, but it was just as embarassing.

As I scrambled for something to put around my waist, my friends finally took a break from their laughing to help me. I was desperate, and I couldn't believe that even Allyce didn't have an extra hoodie or jacket. Finally, someone found a trench coat I could use. Let me tell you, this thing was ugly. But I didn't care, because it would cover up the hole in my pants and keep my underwear from bringing a little extra "pink" to everyone on the parking lot.

This chapter is devoted to those of us who need a little extra coverage, whether it is a sporty vest, a simple shrug for a park outing, or a long coat on the off-chance that you get caught with a hole in your pants. So, get on it, and cover up!

– Nicole

NY Metropolitan
— TRENCH COAT —

Begin with this trench coat

Supplies:

» 1 trench coat
» 1 yd. fabric in a complementary color/pattern for trim
» Thread to match the trench coat
» Covered button kit (number and size to fit buttonholes on trench)
» Belt buckle (optional)
» Safety pin

Designer's Note:

To duplicate a runway look, find fabrics that are close replicas of those used by your favorite designers. Spruce up an old outfit by using these new fabrics to trim a skirt, shirt, jacket or coat.

Instructions

Bottom Ruffle:

1 Unbutton the trench coat. Measure bottom edge of trench from one front to the opposite front side. From the trim fabric, cut enough 8"-wide strips to create one long piece approximately twice the measurement of the bottom of trench. Place the strips with 8" sides right sides together, and seam to make one long trim piece. (Note: the long trim piece will end up being twice as long as the measurement of the bottom edge of the trench.) Finish raw edges with a zigzag stitch.

2 Baste ½" down from the upper raw edge of the trim strip all the way across, leaving extra thread on each end for a tail. Then baste again, this time ¼" down from the upper raw edge, across the trim strip, leaving extra thread on each end for a tail.

3 Stitch a ½" rolled hem on the bottom edge of the fabric, and on both short sides. Press hems.

4 Gently pull the thread tails, gathering the fabric piece to fit the bottom edge of the trench.

5 Using a seam ripper, open up the bottom hem of the trench.

6 Match the hem raw edge to the gathered ruffle trim, wrong sides together. Stitch a ⅝" seam. Fold the hem over the raw edge of the ruffle, and re-sew the hem back together. Press hem.

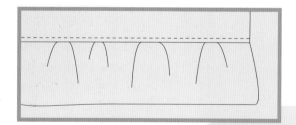

Sleeve Ruffles:

1 Measure around the hem of the trench sleeve, and double this measurement. Cut two pieces of trim fabric 8½" wide and the length of the above measurement.

2 On the top and bottom edge of each piece, stitch a ½" rolled hem and press. To gather the edge, make two lines of basting stitches, one ½" down, and one ¾" down, from the top edge, leaving extra thread for tails. Pull the tails to gather the fabric to fit the sleeve measurement.

3 Right sides together, seam the short edges into a tube and press seam open.

4 Turn right-side out, and pin each sleeve ruffle to the inside of the trench sleeve, adjusting gathers to fit. Attach the ruffle by topstitching over the top of the existing sleeve hem. Repeat for the other sleeve.

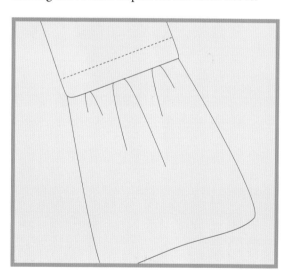

Dilemma:

Having problems keeping the covered button covered? Does the fabric keep slipping off? Try using a spray adhesive to help you out. Spray a light, thin coat over the button, let it sit for about 45 seconds, and then smooth your fabric over the button. This will allow you to tuck the sides of the fabric under without it sliding all over the place.

Collar Trim:

1 Measure the width of the collar. Cut a piece of trim fabric 2½" more than the collar width by 2" wide.

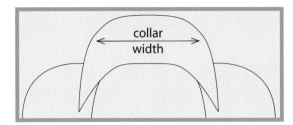

2 Fold the trim strip in half lengthwise, right sides together. Pin and sew seam to create a tube. Press seam open. Using a safety pin, turn the tube right-side out. Center the seam on the tube, and press. Tuck in raw ends. Stitch close to each end, securing the edges.

3 Pin the finished trim strip to the top collar edge, leaving an even amount of excess fabric on each end. Fold under the excess trim on each end. Stitch close to all edges of the trim, securing the trim to the collar.

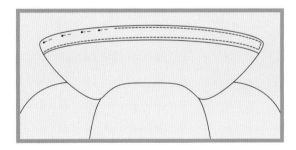

Belt:

1 Measure your waist and add 16" for the length of the belt. Cut a piece of trim fabric that is 8" wide and the length of the belt. Fold strip in half lengthwise, right sides together. Stitch seam on long edge and one short end; press seams open. Clip corner. Turn the belt right-side out. Fold the seam allowances under on the open end; press. Topstitch ⅛" from the edge around all outside edges of the belt. Attach a belt buckle to one end if desired, following the directions on the package.

Placket Trim and Buttons:

1 Measure the width of the placket (front center) on the front of the trench. Add 1½" to this measurement for the seam allowances. Cut two strips from the trim fabric this width by 12" (approximately enough length to cover up to the third button and buttonhole, and the side edges of the collar).

2 Fold the trim strip in half lengthwise, right sides together. Pin and sew seam to create a tube. Press seam open. Using a safety pin, turn the tube right-side out. Center seam on tube and press. Tuck in raw ends. Stitch close to each end, securing the edges.

3 Pin fabric trim strips into place on each placket edge of trench, overlapping fabric trim on collar. Leave excess trim at collar edge. Fold under raw edges to be even with collar edge. Stitch close to all edges of the trim, securing the trim to the collar.

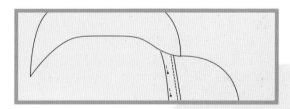

4 Using the covered button kit, cover buttons in trim fabric. Sew buttons into place down the front of the trench.

Tip:

Many of us have the same problem: you can only get one coat for the season, but you don't want to get a black coat because it will clash with brown outfits, and vice versa. Try shopping for a coat in a color like red, green, pink or blue. Choose a color that looks good on you, and you'll never have to worry about whether your browns or blacks are mismatched.

Street Fair

— SHRUG —

Begin with this cardigan

Currently listening to

"Mouth" by Merril Bainbridge

Supplies:

» 1 cardigan
» ⅛"-wide narrow elastic
» 10 buttons for trim
» Matching thread

Designer's Note:

Sometimes mistakes aren't mistakes at all — they are design opportunities! When you cut something too short or it doesn't turn out like you thought it would, sit back and rethink the initial idea. Try to find a way around the problem, and it might turn out to be one of your favorite projects. Don't be afraid to try something crazy!

Instructions

Shrug:

1 Mark where you want the bottom of the cardigan to end; then add ⅝". Cut the cardigan following this marking.

2 Fold up the bottom of the cardigan ⅝". Press in place. Stitch close to the raw edge to form hem.

3 Turn the cardigan inside out, and mark a line lengthwise on each front side, 2" from the button placket (front center of the shirt on one side) and the buttonholes on the other side. Each line should extend from the lower edge of the cardigan up to 1" from the neckline.

4 Mark another line lengthwise on each side front, 3" from each of the first lines.

5 Continue marking lines lengthwise, spacing them 3" apart, until the lines are spaced evenly across the side and back of your cardigan.

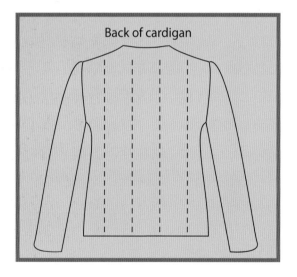

Back of cardigan

6 On the first line on the inside front of the cardigan, pin a piece of elastic at the top of the mark. Leave some excess elastic at the top, and zigzag stitch the elastic down from top to bottom, ending just above the hem. Make the zigzag stitch wide and long so you don't stitch through the elastic. The zigzag stitching will form a casing for the elastic.

7 Using a straight stitch, sew across the top end of the elastic two or three times to secure it in place. Pull on the elastic at the bottom, gathering the cardigan to the desired length. Pin, and stitch the bottom of the elastic to secure. Cut excess elastic off. Repeat for each marked line. This forms the ruching and transforms the cardigan into a shrug.

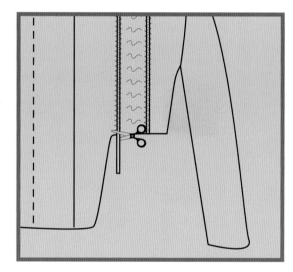

8 Sew buttons at the top of each ruched line of elastic, at the neckline.

Dilemma:
Having trouble keeping the ruching even all around the shrug? When you are gathering the elastic, make sure that the lengths of the gathers (ruching) are all the same by measuring each elastic strip with a tape measure before you cut the elastic to length. And if the measurements are a little bit off, don't worry — no one will ever notice.

Tip:

Do you have a bigger bust, or a not-big-enough bust? Cropped jackets are great for hiding or giving a bigger illusion to the bust area. For those of you with bigger busts, try longer, looser cropped jackets that stop right above where your natural waistline ends. Dark colors are best for diminishing a larger bust. For those of you with smaller busts, try to accentuate it with a fitted, shorter crop jacket that comes just below your bust line. Also, a lighter color, such as a pastel, will give the illusion of a bigger bust line.

Forest Park

—SPORTS VEST—

Begin with this zip-front hooded jacket

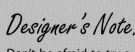

Currently listening to *"Jack and Diane" by John Cougar Mellencamp*

Supplies:

» Semi-fitted zip-front hooded jacket or sweatshirt
» 2½ yd. 2"-wide lace trim
» Matching thread
» 60 small rhinestones (approximately — the number will depend on your jacket)
» Heat-set rhinestone tool

Designer's Note:

Don't be afraid to try a look that your mother or grandmother might wear. The great thing about creating your own clothes is that you get to style them any way you want. A vest doesn't have to have a teddy bear embellished on it! All it needs is a little lace and some "bling," and you've got a young, trendy look.

Instructions

Sports Vest:

1 Mark the sleeves ⅝" past the sleeve seam (for the facing), and cut off excess sleeve. Fold the seam allowance under, forming a facing, and topstitch around the sleeve opening.

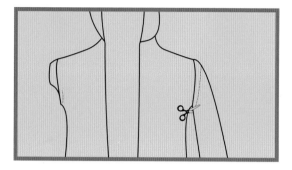

2 Using the lace trim, pin around the armhole, starting at the underarm seam. Fold the lace in half to form a binding around the armhole. One half of the lace will be on the topside of vest, and the other half will be underneath. Pin in place around the armhole. Fold under the raw edge of the lace at the beginning and end, stopping at the underarm side seam. Zigzag stitch through both layers of the lace, being sure to catch both the top and underside of the lace binding.

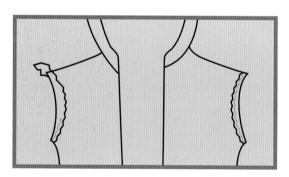

3 Pin the lace to the bottom front of the vest, ⅛" away from the bottom edge, folding in the raw edges of the lace along the front at the zipper. Zigzag stitch along the top and bottom edge of the lace, going around the bottom of the vest.

4 Mark placement for rhinestones, 1" apart, starting at the bottom of the vest along the top of the lace edge. Space marks evenly around the the zipper edge, continuing to mark up the sides of the zipper and all around the edge of the hood.

5 Position the rhinestones along the marks and heat set, following the heat-set tool's directions.

Dilemma:
If you can't find a lace that coordinates well with your jacket, buy plain white cotton lace and dye it. Any fabric dye should do. Follow the instructions on the box, and you'll always have the color you want, whenever you want!

Tip:

We've all considered the age-old question: can I match jean jackets with my jeans? As a rule of thumb, if it doesn't come from the same store and isn't in the same wash, you probably shouldn't be wearing jean jackets with jeans. This look may have been cool in the early 90's, but it's not today.

top it off
— Tops —

It was one of those nights: the kind where no matter what you do, you can't focus on things that really need to get done, like homework. Then again, when you've been working on drawing, draping and pattern-making for hours, you tend to get a little burned out. It was Friday night, and I was at home while everyone else was out and about, going to the movies, having dinner, or doing just about anything other than homework.

I decided that I would procrastinate, like any normal, studious, college student, and rent a movie to watch with my boyfriend. The only problem was that all of the good movies were rented, so we ended up watching TV. Since it was almost midnight, there was obviously nothing good on, or at least nothing we could agree on. I wanted to watch the re-run of the past week's Project Runway, and my boyfriend, like any typical male, wanted to watch Sports Center. So we had a tickle war.

The next morning, I got up to get ready. My boyfriend and I had to be at Grandma's house for dinner in a few hours. As I walked into the bathroom, my heart sank. All over my neck were red spots the size of quarters! Running into my bedroom, I ransacked my closet to find a turtleneck. Perfect! There was only one problem — it was 90 degrees outside, and Grandma would be very suspicious. So, taking an old T-shirt and another old, comfy shirt, I decided to make a short-sleeved scrunched-neck T-shirt. When we arrived at her house, Grandma questioned the unusual look. I simply replied, "It's the latest thing Grandma; I made it myself."

We all have bad luck sometimes. It's a well-known fact that when you think nothing can go wrong, something always will. Whether you need to cover up silly little mishaps on your neck, or you need something quick and simple to spruce up your wardrobe, the shirts in this chapter are sure to suit you well. From an easy reversible tube top that will fit any event to a casual sweater for a night with the girls, you can't go wrong with these combinations. So go ahead, knock 'em out.

– Allyce

Rocker's Fest

— TEE —

Currently
listening to

"Bring You Down" by Taking Back Sunday

Begin with this graphic T-shirt

Supplies:

» 1 fitted graphic T-shirt (main T-shirt)
» XL colored T-shirt (scrap T-shirt for turtleneck and sleeves)
» Thread to match the main T-shirt

Designer's Note:

When you are window-shopping in the mall, don't just wish you could have that shirt in the window — take a good look at it, and see how it's made. Nine times out of ten, you'll be able to duplicate it yourself and save some cash. Plus, you can make whatever color and size you want.

Instructions

Scrunched Turtleneck:

1 Cut the sleeves off the main T-shirt, following the sleeve armhole. Leave a ⅝" seam allowance on each sleeve. Set sleeves aside.

2 Turn the main T-shirt inside-out, with the inside front facing up on the table. Use a seam ripper to carefully remove the ribbing on the neckline of the main T-shirt. Set the ribbing aside. Measure this neckline, and note the measurement.

3 Lay the scrap T-shirt on a table. Cut the back panel out, cutting up both side seams from the hem to the armhole. Then, cut straight across the armhole to make a rectangular piece. Cut a rectangle the width of the neckline measurement (from Step 2) and the length of the cut piece from the T-shirt back. Fold the back panel lengthwise, right sides together, and seam to make a tube. Press seam open. Wrong sides together, pull the top half of the tube down over the bottom of the tube, making sure that the raw edges and seam edges match. This makes your turtleneck.

4 Turn the main T-shirt inside out, and place the turtleneck inside. Match up the raw edges of turtleneck to the raw edges of the main T-shirt neckline, with the turtleneck seam matching to the shoulder seam. Pin the turtleneck in place at the neckline. Stitch ⅝" seam around the neckline. Press seam down toward the T-shirt.

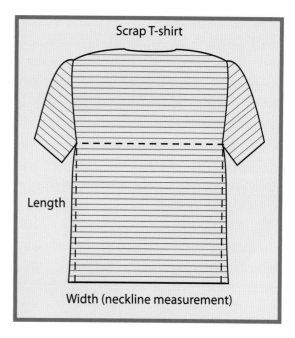

Scrap T-shirt

Length

Width (neckline measurement)

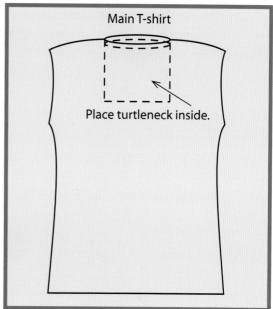

Main T-shirt

Place turtleneck inside.

Dilemma:
Is the turtleneck not fitting over your head? You can try to use a smaller seam allowance, such as ¼" or ½", to give the fabric more room. If this still does not work, try a different shirt with a stretchier fabric (such as Spandex or Lycra).

Sleeves:

1 Measure the raw edge of the sleeve seam cut from the main T-shirt. Note this as Measurement 1. Measure from the top of the sleeve to the hem, and subtract 2". Note this as Measurement 2. Cut a piece of fabric from the scrap T-shirt, the width of Measurement 1 and the length of Measurement 2, and be sure to add a ⅝" seam allowance all around. Cut two of these rectangles.

2 Hem one long side of each rectangle piece, pressing up ½", and stitch close to the edge. Right sides together, sew the side seam and press.

3 Lay the main T-shirt sleeve on top of the new sleeve piece, matching the fold, seam and upper raw edge. Using the main T-shirt sleeve as a pattern, cut a sleeve cap.

4 Place the main T-shirt sleeve inside the new sleeve. Turn the main T-shirt inside out. With the main T-shirt inside-out, place the new "double" sleeve inside the shirt, and match raw edges and seams to the sleeve hole. Your layers should be T-shirt sleeve, new sleeve, T-shirt sleeve hole. Stitch seam and press.

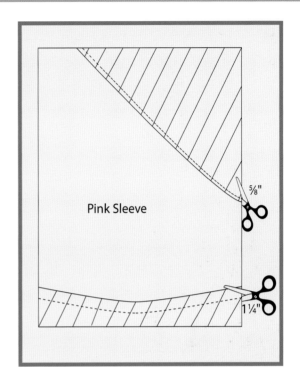

Pink Sleeve

⅝"

1¼"

Add fabric with a great print

Tip:

If you love wearing turtlenecks but you have a short neck, try wearing cowl-neck sweaters. Cowl necks scoop in the front and expose a little collarbone. This will give the illusion that you have a longer neckline, while still allowing you to wear a turtleneck look.

Ivy League Tuxedo

— SHIRT —

Begin with this scoopneck tee

Supplies:

» 1 close-fitting scoopneck or crewneck (rounded neckline) knit top
» 1 tuxedo-style shirt with collar and button front
» ½ yd. fabric (for sash) in a color/ pattern that complements the fitted shirt and tuxedo shirt
» Thread to match fabric
» Buttons (sized to fit existing buttonholes)

Designer's Note:

Mix it up, and wear two garment styles that wouldn't normally go together. Even if one is normally conservative or professional, and the other is fun and casual, sometimes opposites do attract!

Instructions

Top:

1 Lay the knit top flat on the table, with front facing up. Measure your knit top and the yoke of the tuxedo shirt. Measure from shoulder seam to opposite shoulder seams on both knit top and tuxedo shirt. Make sure the measurements are similar so the yoke will fit on the top. If the yoke is too wide, cut it down to fit the width of the knit top.

2 Cut out the yoke on the front of the tuxedo shirt, making sure to keep the collar intact. Leave a ⅝" seam allowance all around the yoke, including the button placket. Continue to cut into the back of the shirt, leaving a ⅝" seam allowance when cutting around the base of the collar.

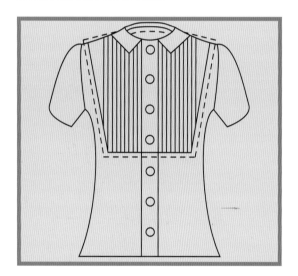

3 Press under ⅝" around the outside edge of the tuxedo yoke.

4 Right sides together, pin the back collar of the tuxedo yoke onto the back neckline of the knit top.

5 On the knit top, use a seam ripper to carefully open both shoulder seams all the way to where the sleeve meets the shoulder seam.

6 Right sides together, pin the shoulder edge of the tuxedo yoke to the back of the knit top shoulder seam allowance. Stitch seam.

7 Lay the knit top out flat on the table, right-side up. Position the tuxedo yoke on top of the knit top. Make sure the tuxedo yoke is buttoned. Pin around the outside edges of the yoke, catching only the top layer of the knit top. Be careful not to pin through to both sides of the knit top — pin only the front.

8 Stitch around the yoke, close to the outside edges.

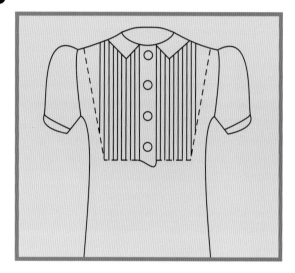

9 Turn the knit top inside out, and cut away excess fabric from the front of the tee, where the yoke was stitched on. Trim near stitching, leaving a ⅝" seam allowance.

10 Remove the old buttons, and sew the new buttons in place on the tuxedo yoke.

Dilemma:
Is the bottom of the placket not lining up properly? Starting on one far side of the insert, sew in toward the placket, but do not sew over the placket yet. Then, on the opposite side of the insert, sew in toward the placket, again not sewing the placket down. Sew the placket last, making sure that the layers overlap and meet perfectly in the middle.

Sash:

1 To make the sash, cut two strips of fabric 9" x 40". Place pieces right sides together, and stitch one 9" end. Press seam open.

2 Fold sash in half lengthwise. Right sides together, match edges, and then stitch ⅝" seam down the long side, and one end of the sash. Clip corners. Turn the sash right-side out. Tuck in the seam allowance on the other end, pin, and press. Topstitch close to the edges, all around the outside edge of the entire sash.

Use a tuxedo shirt with a collar

Tip:
Layered looks are great, but be careful not to get too layered. Tons of layers look great on that size-zero model, but for some of us, size zero passed us up in the eighth grade. For a cute, layered look that won't make you look bulky, buy a couple of tank tops in a coordinating color and wear them under a rectangular, silhouetted jacket.

Work to Play
— REVERSIBLE TUBE —

Begin with this rib-knit sweater vest

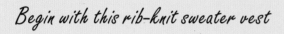

Supplies:

» 1 rib-knit sweater or sweater vest (for bands)
» ⅝ yd. each of 2 different "silky-type" fabrics (tube)
» Matching thread
» ⅝"-wide elastic; measure to fit above bust
» 1"-wide elastic; measure to fit at waist

Designer's Note:

One of our goals is to re-create designer looks for less — but why not also make a look versatile? One simple way to do this is to make the item reversible so you can get two looks out of one piece of clothing. You can save money, time and closet space!

Instructions

Top and Bottom Bands:

1 Using the sweater or sweater vest, cut off a 3½"-wide piece all the way across the bottom of the sweater (ribbing part); cut a continuous circle to use for the top band.

2 Cut off another 3"-wide piece through the cables or center part of the sweater, keeping it in a continuous circle to use for the bottom band.

Body of Tube:

1 Cut two 20" x 22" pieces of each fabric.

2 Pin two pieces (from the same fabric) right sides together, matching the long edges. Stitch a ⅝" seam along long edges. Repeat for the second two pieces from the other fabric. Zigzag stitch to finish the side seams. Press seams open.

3 Wrong sides together, place one fabric "tube" inside of the other, matching the raw edges at the top and bottom, and side seams. Baste around the upper and lower edges, securing the "tubes" together.

4 Using the sweater bands, pin the top band raw edge on the upper raw edge of the tube, right sides together. Stitch ⅝" seam around the top of the band. Fold the band over the raw edge, and pin the edge to the opposite side. Stitch close to the edge, catching both front and back edges of the band. Leave an opening to insert elastic.

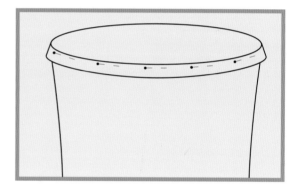

5 Pin the bottom band on the lower raw edge of the tube; complete as described in Step 4.

6 Thread ⅝"-wide elastic through the top band opening, pulling elastic to fit. Stitch the ends together. Thread 1"-wide elastic through the bottom band. Pull the elastic to fit, and stitch the ends together.

7 Hand-stitch or machine stitch the top and bottom band openings closed.

Dilemma:
Are you stitching off the edge when topstitching a casing for elastic? When pinning the edges, pin through the stitching line on the other side of the fabric. Follow the pins as your stitching guide on the right side, removing the pins as you go.

Girl's Night Off
— SWEATER —

Begin with this sweater

Supplies:

» 1 crewneck or turtleneck long-sleeve bulky sweater

» Matching thread

» ¼ yd. fusible knit interfacing

» 3½ yd. ⅜"-wide coordinating satin ribbon

» 1¼ yd. ⅝"-wide coordinating satin ribbon

» Tapestry needle

Designer's Note:

You can find lots of ideas for projects from TV shows movies. Watch your favorite fashion-forward character, and mimic her style. Choose some of the simpler pieces she wears, and put your own spin on them with ribbon, ties or rhinestones. We love Ann Hathaway in "The Devil Wears Prada," which prompted this look.

Instructions

Cutting the Sweater:

1 Look at the neckline of the sweater, and decide which part you want to cut off (ours was cut about 1" below the neck seam). Cut it into a wide neckline. The sweater neckline should hit at the sides of your shoulders.

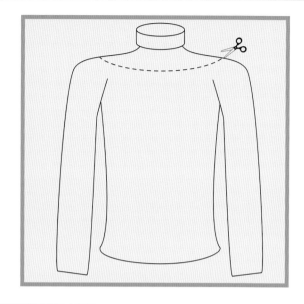

Neck:

1 Cut 2"-wide fusible interfacing strips the length of the cut neckline diameter. Turn the sweater inside out, and iron interfacing on the inside of the sweater neckline edge, letting a tiny bit of the interfacing hang off the cut edge.

2 Zigzag stitch ¼" away from the raw edge, around neckline. Trim off excess interfacing from the edge. Fold the neck over ⅝" to the wrong side, and zigzag the edge in place around the neckline.

3 Using a tapestry needle threaded with the ⅜"-wide ribbon, whipstitch the ribbon around the neckline of the sweater, starting and ending at the shoulder. Tie ribbon ends together on back side of neckline, where ribbon ends meet. Turn sweater right-side out.

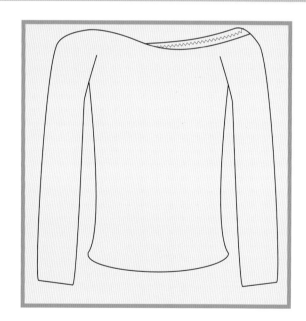

Dilemma:

If you have trouble sewing on the bulky sweater, make your zigzag stitches longer and wider. This will help you get over the bumps in the sweater, and the machine won't get hung up with stitches piling up in one place.

Bottom and Sleeves:

1 Thread tapestry needle with ⅝"-wide ribbon. Starting at the front side, 2" above the bottom edge of sweater, weave ribbon in and out, spacing the "stitches" about 1" apart. Leave 10" of excess ribbon at each end, and tie the loose ends into a bow.

2 Repeat Step 1 for each sleeve, placing the ribbon trim approximately 4" from the bottom edge of each sleeve. Tie the loose ribbon ends together on the backside of each sleeve, where ribbon ends meet.

Tip:
Stripes are a staple for every wardrobe; just make sure that you're wearing the right kind. Wide, horizontal stripes are a very hard look to pull off. They give the illusion that you are wider than you really are. If you like the horizontal look, go for a thin, minimal stripe in a light or pastel color. Vertical stripes are great for adding length to a short waist, and they will make you look longer on top.

bottomed out
— Bottoms —

Christmas is my favorite time of year. It's not about the presents — it's about being with family. This past Christmas, my aunt did something a little different. Instead of giving me the usual, a card with money or a gift card, she decided to buy something for me from this "really hip" clothing boutique. As I opened the gift, she told me, "The saleswoman said all the girls are wearing these again."

Again?! Oh, those dreadful words. I pulled the gift out of the box and gave my aunt a huge smile. "I love it! Oh my gosh, I've been wanting skirt overalls!" I said.

They were awful. I felt like I was 14 again. "You'll look so adorable in them!" My aunt announced. I thought, "Make that 5".

So, after Christmas, I threw the overalls on a hanger and stashed them in the back of my closet. As luck would have it, a few months later, Mom and Dad decided to take a trip to see my aunt and uncle. Mom, of course, thought it would be nice for me to wear what my aunt had given me for Christmas. I called Allyce and begged for her help to transform the overalls into something wearable and trendier. With some excess fabric and a few snips here and there, we created an outfit that wasn't quite so "little girl."

With a sleek, long-sleeve shirt, a pair of leggings and a really hot pair of stilettos, the outfit looked immaculate! When my aunt greeted us at the door of their house she was so excited to see me in the overalls she had given me for Christmas. "Did you do something different to that? I don't remember it looking that way," she asked.

"Oh, I just added a few touches to make it my own," I replied.

Everyone has gotten a horrible outfit for Christmas, but you can use it to create something great. This chapter shows you how to make those dull pants or outdated overalls into something that will attract attention — in a good way. There's even a project for using fabric scraps. You're going to look great the next time you leave your house — and your aunt won't know what happened to those overalls!

– Nicole

Coffee House

— OVERALLS —

Begin with these skirt overalls

Currently listening to *"Crooked Teeth" by Death Cab for Cutie*

Supplies:

» 1 pair of skirt overalls
» 1 yd. coordinating fabric
» Matching thread

Designer's Note:

Remember that fashion happens in a cycle; what is in today won't be in a few months from now, but it will probably be back in 10, 15 or even 20 years. Take a spin on a retro look, and add your own modern style. You never know — you might narrow that 20-year cycle down to 10 with your ingenuity!

Instructions

Bib Overalls:

1 Cut the top (bib) off the overalls ⅝" above the waistline seam. (This is your ⅝" seam allowance for attaching the new bib.) Cut the upper band from the bib, ⅝" below the riveted buttons. Set aside. Remove the pocket from the bib you just cut off, using a seam ripper to carefully take out the stitches. Set this pocket aside.

2 Use the cut overalls bib as a pattern for making the new bib. Lay the bib on the fabric, with the fabric folded right sides together. Trace around the edge of the bib. Add ⅝" seam allowances all around. Cut the fabric.

3 Right sides together, stitch around the sides and upper edge, leaving the bottom edge open. Trim the corners. Turn right-side out, carefully poking out the corner edges. Press. Topstitch ¼" away from the edge all the way around the side and top bib edge.

4 Pin the bib pocket in the center of the new bib. Stitch around the sides and bottom of the pocket, attaching it to the bib.

5 Pin the new bib to the overalls skirt bottom, attaching the bib lower edge to the waist seam of the skirt seam allowance, right sides together. Stitch ⅝" seam, and finish seam edge with a zigzag stitch.

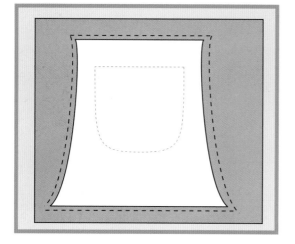

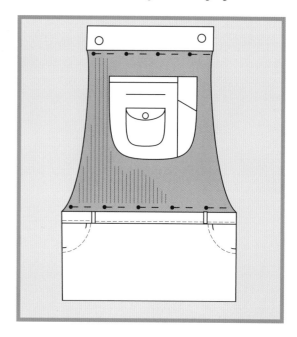

Dilemma:
Is your machine needle breaking on denim? Use a jean needle. It is a little larger and thicker, designed specifically to go through denim and heavier fabrics like canvas easily.

Ruffles:

1 Cut off the bottom of the overalls skirt right above the ruffle seam line. If there is no ruffle, only cut off the hem of the skirt.

2 Measure how much longer you want the finished skirt of the overalls to be, once the ruffle has been added. This measurement plus 2" for seam allowances is the width you will cut your two ruffle pieces.

3 Next, measure the circumference of the bottom edge of the skirt. Double this circumference measurement. Using the width determined in Step 2, cut two pieces from the fabric to make the length necessary for the ruffle.

4 Pin the two fabric pieces right sides together, and stitch ⅝" seam on both short sides to make a tube.

5 On one raw edge, stitch two rows of basting stitches, one at ¼" and one at ½". Pull on the threads to gather. Gather the ruffle to fit the lower edge of the skirt.

6 Pin the ruffle to the bottom edge of the skirt, right sides together, and stitch ⅝" seam. Finish seam edges.

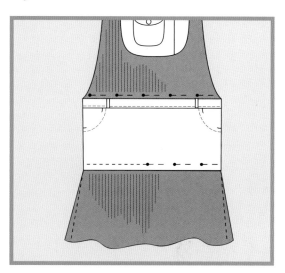

7 For the hem, turn under the bottom edge of the ruffle ⅝" twice; press. Stitch close to the edge.

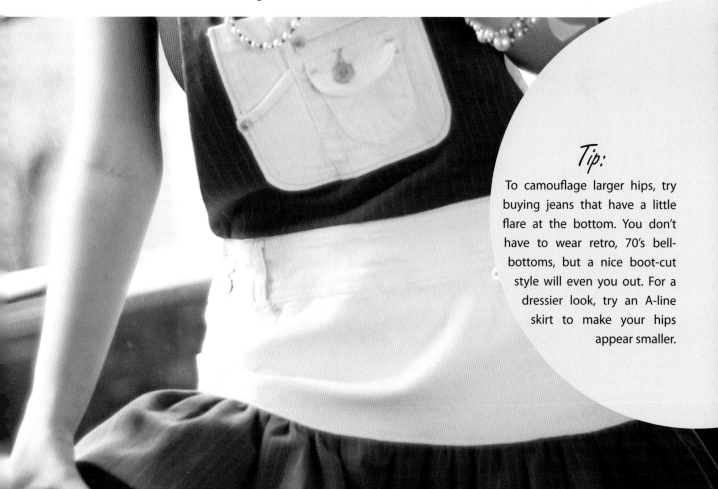

Tip:

To camouflage larger hips, try buying jeans that have a little flare at the bottom. You don't have to wear retro, 70's bell-bottoms, but a nice boot-cut style will even you out. For a dressier look, try an A-line skirt to make your hips appear smaller.

Boardwalk

— SKIRT —

Currently
listening to

"Down On The Corner" by Credence Clearwater Revival

Supplies:

» ¼ yd. each (approximately) of several different patterned fabrics (use up your scraps!)
» 1 yd. ¾"-wide elastic
» ½ yd. gridded tracing paper

Designer's Note:

Don't be afraid to create your own pattern. Basic pattern-making is just connecting the dots, something we all learned in elementary school. Plot the points from the grid design on 1" gridded tracing paper, and then connect the dots to get a pattern piece. It's a simple way to make non-fitted garments. To learn more, pick up a basic pattern-making book.

Instructions

Pattern and Cutting:

1 Print the pattern piece from the CD. Cut out pattern piece.

2 Measure your hips. Add 3" to this measurement for ease. Use this measurement to determine how many strip pieces to cut from your scraps.

Size	Hip Measurement + 3"	Strips Needed
Extra Small	34"	17
Small	36"	18
Medium	38"	19
Large	40"	20
Extra Large	42"	21

Piecing and Sewing:

1 Lay the strips in an order that you like. Avoid placing two of the same fabric strips too close to each other, and vary the light and dark pieces.

2 Place the first two strips right sides together, matching the long edges, and stitch a ⅝" seam along one long edge. Press seam open. Finish seam edges with a zigzag stitch.

3 Continue adding strips, seaming right sides together until you have pieced all the strips into a long rectangle.

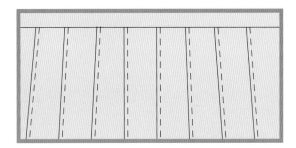

4 With right sides together, stitch the first strip sewn to the long edge of the last strip. You will have a tube-like piece now.

5 Finish the top and bottom edges with a zig-zag stitch.

6 At the upper edge of the skirt, fold over 1½" to the inside of the skirt, and stitch close to the finished edge to create the casing. Leave a 3" opening for elastic. Insert elastic. Pull to fit waist, and cut off excess. Overlap the elastic ends and stitch. Straight stitch the elastic opening closed.

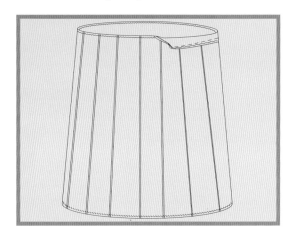

7 At the hem edge of skirt, turn the edge up 1", and topstitch close to the finished edge by machine or slipstitch the hem by hand.

Dilemma:

Do you have strips of colored fabric that don't really coordinate? Try finding a neutral color to put in between the two colors that don't seem to work. This way, the colors are not "fighting hues" directly next to one another.

Tip:

To make short legs look longer, wear straight jeans that are a little longer than your normal length to cover over your shoes. This extra inch or two will make you look taller.

Not-So-Knickerbocker

— CAPRIS —

Begin with these tweed pants

Currently
listening to

"Walk This Way" by Aerosmith

Supplies:

» 1 pair of tailored wool tweed pants
» ½ yd. contrasting wool fabric
» Matching thread

Designer's Note:

Scissors can be your best friend when you want to change things up a bit. Subtraction is an easy way to transform something you wouldn't wear in public into something spectacular.

Instructions

Capris:

1 Try on the pants, and mark 1" below the kneecap. Take the pants off, and draw a straight line across the front and back at that point. Cut off the bottom of the pants at the point marked.

2 Measure the circumference of the pant leg and add 1¼" seam allowances. Cut two pieces from contrasting fabric this measurement long by 6½" wide. These are the cuff pieces for the capris.

3 On the outer seam of the lower edge of each pant leg, fold three pleats, taking in ½" in each pleat. Pin pleats in place, then baste at the raw edge to hold them in place. Press the pleats about 2" into the pant leg.

4 Fold each cuff piece right sides together, matching the 6½" raw edges, and stitch the seam. Press seam open. Fold the cuff wrong sides together, matching the raw edges, and baste seam edges together.

5 Pin the bottom of each cuff to the bottom of each pant leg, right sides together, matching raw edges. Place the cuff seam to the inside seam of the pant leg. Stitch ⅝" seam and finish edges with a zigzag stitch. Press seam toward the pant leg.

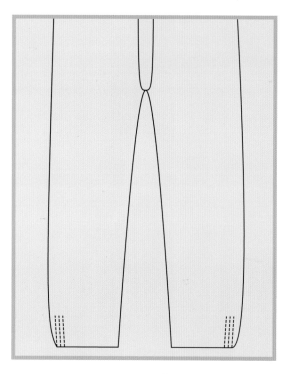

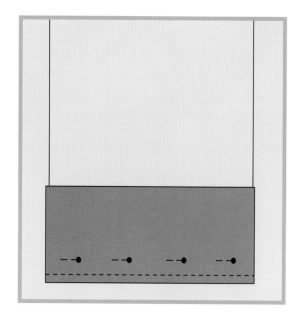

Dilemma:

Turning "tired" pants into something new is inexpensive and easy. Tailored pants, like the ones we used for the Not-So-Knickerbocker Capris, can be restyled into a short skirt, shorts, bermudas, or even a purse or pillow. Nobody will ever know that those cast-off pants had been taking up residence in the dark corner of your closet in their previous life!

Sash:

1 Cut two pieces from contrasting fabric, 7½" x 40".

2 Place pieces right sides together. Stitch one short side with a ⅝" seam, and press open.

3 Fold the sash in half lengthwise, right sides together. Stitch ⅝" seam down one short end and the long side of the sash. Trim corners.

4 Turn right-side out, poke out the corners, and slip-stitch the open end closed.

5 Topstitch a decorative stitch on one long edge, and straight stitch the other remaining sides. Use rows of decorative stitches as desired for trim.

Tip:
If you don't have a can of anti-static spray, try spraying hairspray on the inside of your skirt or pants to get rid of static cling. You don't need much, just a light mist. If you don't want to use hairspray, rub a new dryer sheet on the inside of the skirt or pants. Keep one in your purse for future touch-ups.

icing
— Accessories —

It was ten o'clock on a Saturday morning. "Finally a morning to sleep in and be a bum" I thought. As I lay in bed, eyes closed, I felt someone (or something) jump on the bed. "Nicole, get up!" Allyce said.

She must have a sixth sense or something, because anytime I want to sleep in, she is there to wake me up.

"What?" I murmured into my pillow.

"Let's do something. I'm really bored, and it's so pretty outside."

"Go for a run." I said. "You keep talking about how you need to exercise more."

"Are you saying I'm fat?" Allyce joked. "Come on, let's go shopping."

"One slight problem — we're broke, and I know you ... you're going to see something you want and then buy it, and then have buyer's remorse. Then I will have to listen to you for until we go shopping next weekend, and you buy something else, and have buyer's remorse all over again. It's like this vicious cycle you're on." I sat up and looked at her. She obviously wanted to go badly. "Fine let me throw some clothes on and we'll go," I said.

When we got to the mall, it was jam-packed! As we weaved in and out of the crowds, I followed Allyce into twenty different stores. I'd heard of window-shopping, but this was insane. We had been at the mall for over three hours and she had tried on everything imaginable, including clothes, shoes and the latest must-have accessories. I know Allyce loves shoes, but how many pairs does one girl need?

I thought we would make it out of the mall without the usual buyer's remorse, when she found a designer belt that she couldn't live without. Even I had to agree it was exquisite, but it would cost her a full month's rent. I knew I would never hear the end of it if she bought it, so I suggested, "Why don't you just make it? You can copy that look. That belt is too big anyway, and you could make it so it fits perfectly!" After a long pause, Allyce finally put the belt back, grabbed her purse (and me), and we headed to a fabric store. After purchasing some fabric, doing a little measuring, and some trial-and-error sewing, she had a designer belt that was to die for. With a silky top and a trendy jacket, she had a great outfit.

You can come up with any accessory idea by just window-shopping. That's how we came up with the ideas for our projects in this chapter. We re-created a couple of our favorite looks and made them to fit our tastes. Just think how great you'll feel with a fantastic belt and the perfect bag!

– Nicole

Haute Couture

— REVERSIBLE BELT —

Currently listening to
"Seasons" by Good Charlotte

Supplies:

» 1 belt buckle
» ¼ yd. suede fabric in Color 1
» ¼ yd. suede fabric in Color 2
» 1½ yd. 1½"-wide lace
» 3 packs fusible suede in 3 different colors
» Circle stencil (or use a bottle or small round object to trace circles)

Designer's Note:

When working with clothing articles, don't limit yourself to "sewing tools." Check in your art supply or home tools area for help. An X-acto knife can be the perfect tool for cutting out detailed shapes or designs!

Instructions

Belt Strip:

1 Measure around your waist or hip where you want your belt to sit, and add 7"; this is your belt length.

2 Cut your belt front and back pieces from the two colors of suede fabric. Cut each piece the belt length (determined above) by 3" wide. Cut two lengths from the lace trim, each the length of the belt pieces.

3 On one end of each suede strip, cut the fabric at an angle for the belt point.

Belt Piece:

1 On one belt piece (Color 1), pin the lace along both long edges. Stitch the lace to the belt piece close to each edge and along the scalloped edges.

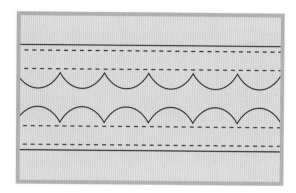

2 Trace circles onto the back of the fusible suede, using a small bottle or other round object. Cut seven circles from each color sheet of the fusible suede. Lay out the design, with one of each color circle overlapping to form the motif. Space the grouped circles evenly along the belt length (Color 2), and fuse in place with iron and press cloth.

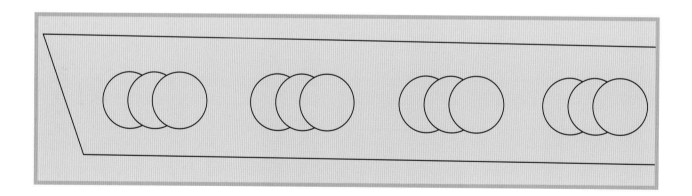

Dilemma:

Do the edges of the reverse side of your belt show when you put it on? Use an iron and press the belt from both sides so the edges are completely even. Topstitch closely around all of the edges to keep the belt edges from rolling over to the wrong side.

3 Right sides together, pin both embellished belt pieces along the long edges. Stitch ⅝" seam, starting along one long edge, down to the point. Start at the short straight end, and then stitch down the other long side. Leave the straight short side open. Trim points.

4 Turn the belt right-side out, and tuck in the raw edges on the open end. Stitch closed, close to edge. Press belt carefully along edges, so that one side does not show onto the other side. Loop the straight end through the belt buckle, overlapping the end far enough to be able to pin to buckle. Stitch across the end.

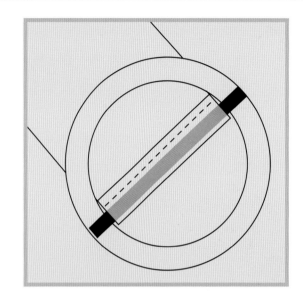

Hampton

— WEEKENDER BAG —

Supplies:

» ½ yd. oxford-striped fabric for bag
» ⅝ yd. pink green ticking stripe for lining and upper band
» Tear-away stabilizer
» 3 yd. ¾"-wide cotton cording
» 4 large grommets and grommet tool (optional)
» Iron-on washable hook-and-loop tape
» Marking pen
» Embroidery thread
» Compass and Letters embroidery designs from the CD

Designer's Note:

Monogrammed lettering can lend a sense of elegance to a project. Mix it up a bit! Monograms can look great on the usual shirts, necklaces and towels, but try adding initials to a beach bag or other casual accessories. Your laid-back project will automatically look upscale!

Instructions

Cutting:

1 Cut two 12" wide by 9" high rectangles of oxford-striped fabric for the bag.

2 Cut two 12" wide by 14" high rectangles of ticking fabric for the bag lining and top band.

3 Cut one 5" x 12" pocket from the ticking fabric.

Construction:

1 Find and mark the center point on the right side of one of the bag pieces. To find the center point, fold the fabric in half crosswise and finger press. Open fabric out, fold in half lengthwise, and finger press. The crossing pressed lines will mark the center of the fabric.

2 Layer the fabric with tear-away stabilizer and place in the embroidery hoop, following directions for your embroidery machine.

3 Embroider a monogram motif as directed in your embroidery machine manual.

4 Pin the two bag pieces with right sides together along the side and bottom edges. Stitch along the pinned edges with a ½" seam allowance. Press seams open.

5 Refold one bottom corner of the bag so the side seam is over the bottom seam. Stitch across the corner 2½" from the point, forming a triangle. Repeat with the other corner to square off the tote bag bottom.

6 Fold the pocket in half with right sides together, matching the 5" edges. Stitch along the side and bottom edges, leaving a small opening for turning. Trim the corners, turn right-side out, and press. Slip stitch the opening closed.

7 Mark the pocket placement on the right side of the lining, centered 6" down from one 12" edge. Pin the pocket at the marking, and edge stitch along the side and bottom edges.

8 Stitch the lining pieces together in the same manner as the bag pieces, leaving a 4" opening in the bottom edge for turning (see Steps 4 and 5).

9 Cut a 6" length of the fabric fusion. Using the loop side of the tape and following the manufacturer's directions, center the tape over the right side of one of the lining side seams. The bottom edge of the tape should be even with the bottom of the seam. Fuse in place.

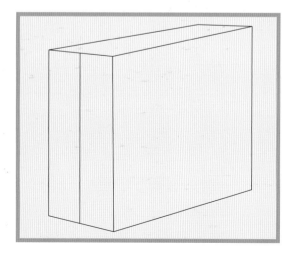

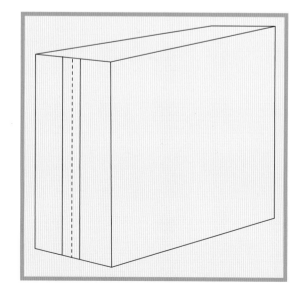

10 Place the bag inside the lining, right sides together. Stitch along the upper edge with a ½" seam allowance. Press the seam toward the lining. Turn the tote bag right-side out through the opening in the lining. Slip stitch the opening closed.

11 Tuck the lining inside the bag so the bottom of the bag and the bottom of the lining meet. The lining will extend beyond the bag. Press along the top edge, and topstitch close to the fold. Stitch again close to the seam.

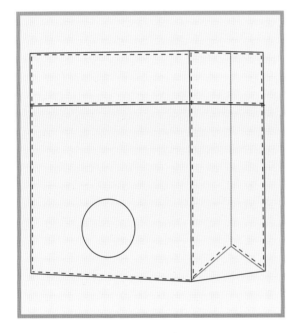

12 Mark the placement of the grommets in the center of the top band, about 4" in from each side seam. Install following manufacturer's directions. (Note: If you prefer, stitch buttonholes rather than using grommets.)

13 Cut two 36" lengths of cord. Tightly wrap tape around the cut end of the cords. Thread the cord from the inside to the outside of the bag, and knot. Clip off the taped end.

Glasses Case

Supplies:

» 6" x 7" piece of main fabric
» 6" x 7" piece of lining fabric
» 6" x 6" piece of fusible batting
» The remaining hook side of the iron-on washable hook-and-loop tape (from the bag lining)

Instructions

Construction:

1 Select the fabric you would like to use as the lining for your eyeglass case, and place this fabric right-side down.

2 Place batting on the wrong side of the lining fabric, ½" in from the edges. Following manufacturer's directions, fuse the batting in place.

3 Fold the main fabric in half crosswise, matching the 7" edges. Finger press. Open the fabric out, and center the hook tape on the right side of the fabric between the fold and the cut edge. Fuse in place.

4 Pin the lining and the main fabric with right sides together, and stitch along all edges with a ½" seam allowance, leaving an opening for turning.

5 Turn right-side out and press; slipstitch the opening closed. Topstitch close to the top edge (one 6" edge).

6 Fold the fabric in half lengthwise, with lining together. Topstitch along the side and bottom edges of the eyeglass case. Attach the case to the inside of the bag along the hook-and-loop tape.

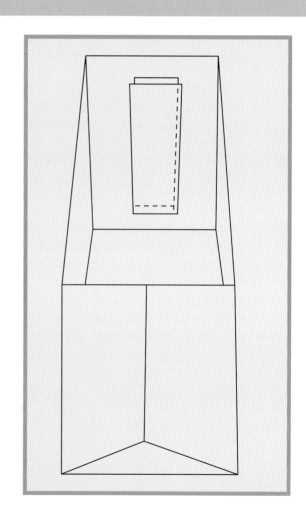

Dilemma:

When embroidering lettering or monograms, be sure that the letters are lined up and centered properly for a professional look. Do your monogram embroidery on a larger fabric piece before cutting and sewing the project. That way, you can work with the piece and adjust the placement of the finished monogram. Cut the piece out, and then assemble your project.

Instructions

Construction:

1 Fold the main piece of fabric in half crosswise, matching the 3½" edges. Stitch along the two side edges with a ½" seam allowance.

2 Press the seam allowance open, and finish the bottom corners as in the beach bag, stitching ¾" in from the points. (Refer to Steps 4 and 5 in the bag instructions.)

3 Repeat with the lining fabric.

4 Set the lining piece aside. Turn the main fabric piece right-side out.

5 Cut a 1" piece of hook-and-loop tape, and fuse one side of the tape over the side seam of the main fabric, placing it 1" from the top edge.

6 Fold the ribbon in half crosswise, and stitch close to each edge. Baste the cut edge of the ribbon to the top edge of the main fabric, centering the ribbon over the side seam opposite the hook-and-loop tape.

7 Place the lining over the main fabric, right sides together. Stitch along the top edge, leaving an opening for turning. Press seam toward the lining.

8 Turn right-side out and press. Topstitch along the top edge, closing the opening.

9 Wrap the ribbon around the handle of the beach bag, and mark the point where it will overlap with the hook-and-loop tape. Fuse the remaining piece of hook-and-loop tape to the inside of the ribbon at the marked point.

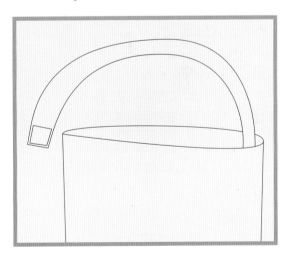

10 Insert your cell phone, and attach the caddy to the handle of the bag.

Tip:

Scarves don't have to be worn around your neck or as a belt. Tie a scarf around your wrist for a new twist on a bracelet, or wrap it around your head for a trendy style. You can even tie a scarf around your purse strap to coordinate with your outfit. The scarf is the chameleon of accessories.

headin' out

— Hair Accessories —

Chapter 6

There was absolutely nothing on TV. I had no work or projects to do, and, of course, there was nothing to watch. Allyce was in the sewing room trying to finish a huge sewing project, when I heard her cell phone ring. Ten minutes later, she came down the stairs with a pad of paper in her hand. I just knew what was coming next.

"Hey Nicole, do you want to go to a party this weekend?" She sat on the coffee table in front of me.

"It depends — does it have a theme?" I asked. All of the parties around here had themes.

"It's a retro 80's party. I thought it would be really fun to go to."

"What do we have to wear? Can we pick anything?"

"Well, I guess. Why?" Allyce asked.

"Remember the last hideous party you took me to?"

"Yeah, where everybody had an ugly 'gifted' sweater on?" she laughed.

It really was a lot of fun, I thought, so why not. "All right, all right, we'll go," I said.

The next day, we tried to figure out what we were going to wear. I had a pair of bright-pink satin spandex pants (I'm not really sure why) and an oversized black shirt. Allyce had a red and black polka dot dress with huge, puffy sleeves. We were definitely set for the 80's part, but there was something missing. We decided we needed headbands and feathered hair.

It was easy to find plain plastic headbands, but we needed them to match our outfits. After raiding the scrap fabric bin in the sewing room, we came up with some perfect finds. An hour later, we had two very large headbands, one with rhinestones and one with a bow. That Friday after class, we relaxed and got ready for the party. When we were finished with our hair, we took a step back and looked in the mirror.

"Nicole?" Allyce asked.

"Yeah?"

"Am I crazy, or do we actually look good, even before we put the whole outfit on?"

"You know, I think I'm going to start wearing headbands more often. I really like this thing," I said as I readjusted the headband in my hair.

We got to the party, and everyone looked just as crazy as we did! As the night progressed, Allyce and I got tons of compliments on our headbands. Who would have thought that a 20-minute project could be so awe-inspiring?

For this chapter, we came up with different headband ideas for easy, fast fashion. Put your personal style into these projects by choosing different fabrics and trims. Heads up — smiles on!

– Nicole

Editorial
— HEADBAND —

Currently listening to

"Wonderwall" by Oasis

Supplies:

» 1 wide plastic headband
» ⅛ yd. cotton print fabric
» Scrap piece of suede fabric for lining
» ½ yd. each, two coordinating colors of wide rickrack
» Fabric glue
» Computer paper and tape
» Stapler
» Clip-style clothes pins or large binder clips

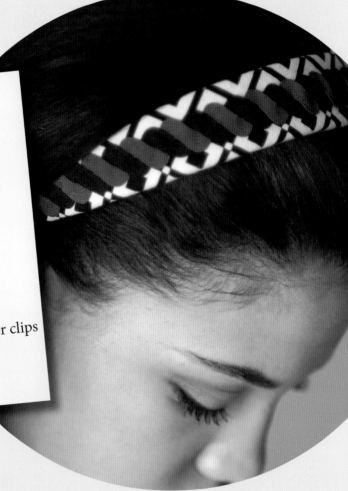

Designer's Note:

You don't need much to turn something plain into something spectacular. Start with a basic plastic headband, and transform it into a fashionable accessory with a simple scrap of fabric. Add trim, and you've got a whole new look!

Instructions

Headband:

1 Tape two pieces of computer paper together. Place one end of the headband flat on the paper, and trace the end. Roll the headband down on paper, and continue to trace and roll until you get down to the other end. Add ½" seam allowance around all sides. Cut out the paper pattern.

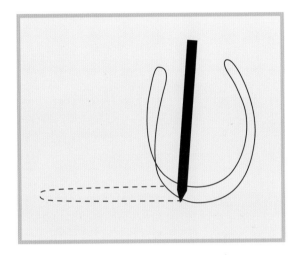

2 Pin the pattern to the cotton fabric, and cut.

3 Cut off the seam allowance on the paper pattern, and pin the pattern to the suede fabric. Cut out the lining piece.

4 Starting on one end of the headband, place just enough glue to cover the headband for about 2". Place the cotton piece on the glue-covered headband. Leave ½" hanging over on each side and end.

5 Continue to glue and smooth fabric until you get to the other end. Place a line of glue on the sides and inside edge of the headband. Fold the fabric over around the side edges to the underside of the headband and let dry.

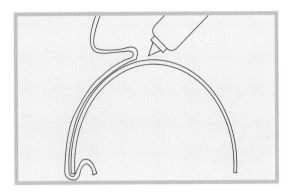

6 Place glue on the inside of the headband, covering the exposed plastic. Place the suede lining on the inside of the headband, starting on one end, and smooth evenly to the other end; let dry.

7 Take each piece of the wide rickrack, and twist together, interlocking the zigzags. Staple each end of the interlocked rickrack to hold the ends together.

8 Glue along the center line of the fabric-covered headband. Leaving about 1" of the twisted rickrack trim on each end, glue the trim piece to the headband. Carefully fold the ends of the trim to the underside of the headband. Glue ends in place, and clip a clothes pin or clip to each end. Let dry, then trim away rick-rack ends and staples.

Dilemma:
Is the glue taking forever to dry? Use clothes pins to hold the fabric or trim in place. This way, you don't have to hold the band together — you can move on to another project while it's drying. Clothes pins are great to keep in your sewing box for other hands-free projects.

Tip:
Ponytails are casual and super-easy to pull off. Play around to find the right style for your facial structure. If you have a broad forehead, throw some bangs into the mix to avoid emphasizing the forehead. If you have a short forehead, slick back your hair and don't wear bangs. Top it off with a headband for a sleek, polished look.

Chain Reaction

— HEADBAND —

Supplies:

» ½ yd. ¼" chain
» ⅛ yd. fabric
» 5" of ¼"-wide elastic
» Pliers (to cut chain)

Designer's Note:

Headbands are a staple in any wardrobe. Many are casual, so try dressing them up with chains and other metal findings for jewelry-like appeal.

Instructions

Headband:

1 Measure the chain to your head by starting at the base of one ear and going over the top of head to the base of the other ear. Cut the chain this length.

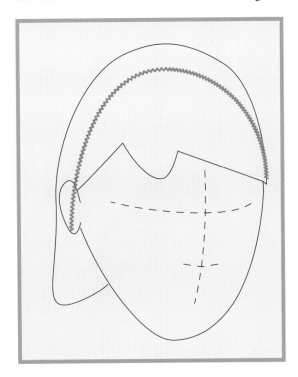

2 Cut fabric 1¾" wide by the length of the chain plus 4".

3 Fold the fabric strip in half lengthwise, wrong sides together, and stitch ½" seam. Zigzag close to the stitching, or serge finish the raw edge. Trim away excess seam allowance.

4 Keeping the raw edge centered in the back, top-stitch through the center of the tube piece.

5 Weave the fabric tube through the chain links in an over-and-under pattern. Leave a ⅝" seam allowance on each end; cut off excess.

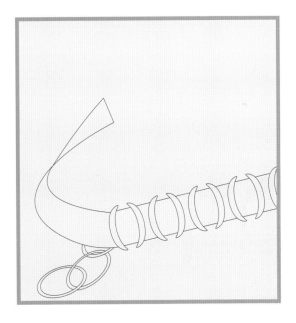

6 Loop elastic through the end of the last link, and pin the elastic to the fabric tube end on each side. Hand-stitch the elastic to the fabric on both ends.

Dilemma:

Having trouble threading the fabric through the chain without it unraveling? Place tape around the end, and thread it through. This will keep the end from raveling and it's easy to remove once you're finished.

Tip:

The trademark of every good make-up artist is creating a natural look. For an easy, everyday look, use golden browns. A brown/bronze on your upper eyelid, a light touch of mascara, bronzer on cheeks and a little bit of clear lip gloss are all you need for a perfect, sun-kissed look.

Art Director
— HEADSCARF —

Supplies:

» ¼ yd. fabric, at least 42" wide
» Small plastic buckle
» Elastic ponytail tie

Designer's Note:

Sometimes the simplest item in your bathroom can make a world of difference in a project. A plain elastic ponytail hair tie makes attaching a buckle to your headscarf easy.

Instructions

Headscarf:

1 Cut a 8" x 40" strip from fabric.

2 Fold the fabric in half lengthwise, right sides together. If desired, cut the end at an angle to make one end go to a point. Pin and stitch a ⅝" seam along the long side and across one end. Clip corners.

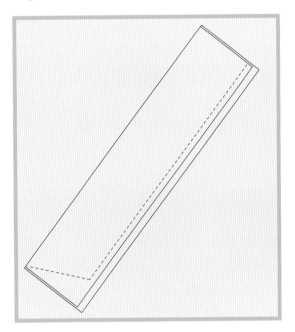

4 Slip one end of the finished scarf through the elastic ponytail tie, folding the fabric end over. Stitch the end to the fabric, securing the scarf to the elastic ponytail tie. Loop the end of the elastic hairband through the center of the buckle, attaching the scarf to the buckle.

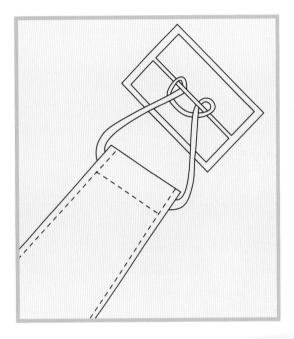

3 Turn the piece right-side out, and fold the remaining raw edge in; press. Topstitch closely around all edges.

Dilemma:
Does the headscarf keep slipping? Use bobby pins and hairspray to prevent it from moving around on your head. Also, a little teasing on the crown of your head will keep the scarf from sliding back; we're not talking about 80's-style teasing here, just enough to get a little volume.

Tip:
A purse is a girl's best friend. Everyone needs at least one or two (or 10, or 12), but a purse shouldn't be a catch-all, carry-all for everything you own. If you've got a lot of stuff that you have to carry around with you, get a larger tote that will accommodate everything, and use a smaller purse for the essentials. The only things you need in your purse are a wallet, a little make-up, and your keys. Save the computer, date book and other stuff for the larger tote. Keep things uncluttered. After all, who wants to be digging endlessly in a bag?

manly gear
— Men's Wear —

A lot of people our age complain about having no money, and each one has his or her own special excuse: "I spent too much at Starbucks, "I lost it in a poker tournament," "I spent it on a much-needed pair of shoes," or "But really, I spent all my cash on food, I swear!" Whatever the reason, we're just broke. So when it comes to buying gifts for those special people in our lives, namely our beaus, we tend to fall a little short of what we really want for them. So why not make something ourselves?

For some, this might be a little intimidating. We can barely get our guys to wear the stuff we buy them, much less get them to wear something we make. So how do you create something that your guy is sure to love? It's easy — make it something ultra simple! Guys want something that's comfortable, that they'll use a lot.

When it came time to get my boyfriend a gift for his birthday, I was running pretty short on cash. It wasn't my fault. I found the last vintage pattern for my collection online. The auction had only 10 minutes left, and if I didn't bid, I may never have finished my collection of Suzy Stephens sewing patterns. But when the auction was over, I was seriously strapped for cash. When I couldn't find anything affordable to get my boyfriend, Nicole and I went window-shopping. Five minutes later, we hit the clearance rack and found a pair of plain boxers. Nicole told me that I was going to have to fix them up or it wouldn't be a very good gift. When we got home, we laid the boxers on the floor. I sat at one end, and Nicole sat at the other. We stared at the boxers for awhile, switched positions, stared a little more, went downstairs, ate peanut butter and jelly sandwiches (brain food), stared a little more, checked MySpace ... well, you get the idea. Finally, a brainstorm hit, and we were off and running with the project. With a small cut of fabric and leftover thread, I made my guy some great boxers that he wouldn't be afraid to wear.

This chapter gives you two ideas for your guy's wardrobe. If you don't have a boyfriend, I'm sure you have a good friend or brother who would enjoy them just as much. Both projects are simple and super-quick to complete, so if you are like me and forget all about a birthday until the night before (come on, you know it happens), you can finish a great gift in no time flat. He'll think you spent hours upon hours making them! So take initiative and show your guy what you're made of!

– Allyce

Luck of the Draw

— BOXERS —

Currently listening to "Mony Mony" by Billy Idol

Begin with these men's boxers

Supplies:

» 1 pair of jersey-knit men's boxers
» ⅛ yd. printed fabric with motif appropriate for cutting appliqué
» 2 shank-style decorative buttons (optional)
» Lightweight computer paper
» Marking pencil

Designer's Note:

Who says that only women can wear fun underwear? Sometimes techniques seen on shirts, jackets or even jeans can be used on boxers.

Instructions

Boxers:

1 Select a motif for the fabric appliqué on the printed fabric. Place the paper on top of the fabric motif, and trace around the outline of the design. Add ½" seam allowance all around, and cut out the pattern.

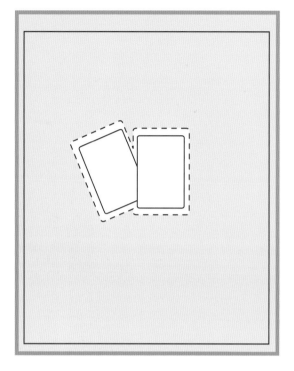

2 Pin the pattern to the fabric motif, and cut the fabric. Set the motif aside.

3 Cut the seam allowances off of the paper pattern. Pin the pattern on a corner of boxers, trace around the pattern, and cut out a "window" for fabric appliqué (be careful not to cut to the end of the boxers).

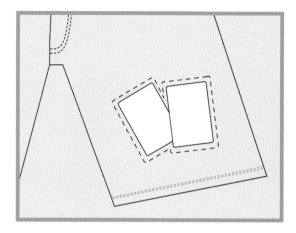

4 Place the fabric cut-out underneath the window on the boxers so you see the whole pattern of the fabric motif. Pin in place.

5 Topstitch ¼" away from the cut edge of the window, attaching the fabric motif to the boxers.

6 Mark the desired placement of the buttons. Hand-stitch the buttons in place.

Dilemma:
Don't know what kind of boxers to use for this project? Any type of jersey-knit boxers will work perfectly. Try to stay away from woven cotton or silk boxers, because they will ravel.

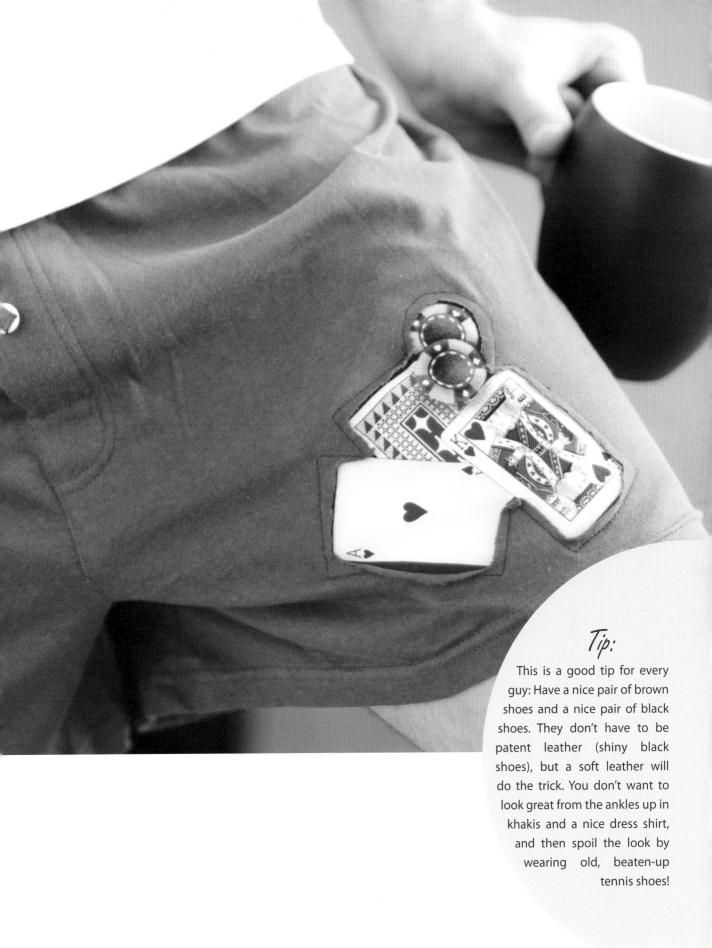

Tip:

This is a good tip for every guy: Have a nice pair of brown shoes and a nice pair of black shoes. They don't have to be patent leather (shiny black shoes), but a soft leather will do the trick. You don't want to look great from the ankles up in khakis and a nice dress shirt, and then spoil the look by wearing old, beaten-up tennis shoes!

Marathon

— SHIRT —

Begin with this Lycra T-shirt

Supplies:

» Men's sport-type Lycra T-shirt
» ¼ yd. of Lycra fabric in a contrasting color
» 4" of ⅛"-wide elastic

Designer's Note:

To find ideas for a project, take a look around you. The things you see every day can suddenly inspire you. Create something that makes an everyday routine easier, such as a place to put your iPod while you run or work out.

Instructions

Cutting:

1 Try on the T-shirt, and mark the desired finished length of the sleeves (how long you want them to be after the cuffs have been added). Add a ⅝" seam allowance, and cut excess off of each sleeve.

2 Lay the T-shirt out flat on the table, and measure the circumference of the bottom of the sleeve. Add 1¼" to this measurement for seam allowances.

3 Cut two pieces from the Lycra fabric, the circumference measurement calculated above by 10".

Construction:

1 Right sides together, match 10" ends of each Lycra piece. Use a zigzag stitch to sew the seam. Trim excess seam allowance. Turn right-side out.

2 Fold each Lycra piece in half, wrong sides together, matching the raw edges; pin. This forms the cuff for each sleeve. Baste the raw edges of each cuff piece together so they don't slip when attaching to sleeve.

3 Attach the cuff to the inside of each sleeve of the T-shirt, wrong side of the T-shirt to the cuff, matching the cuff seam to the underarm seam of the sleeve. Zigzag stitch ⅝" seam. Trim excess seam allowance.

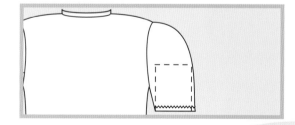

4 Measure the width of your MP3 player. Fold up one cuff over the sleeve, and mark the placement for the stitching lines the width of the MP3 player. Stitch two rows, forming the pocket into which the MP3 player will fit. (Make sure it is a bit narrower than the MP3 player to keep it from slipping out of the pocket — Lycra stretches, and you don't want the MP3 player to fall out.) Repeat for the other pocket, this time marking placement for the stitching lines the width of a credit card or cell phone.

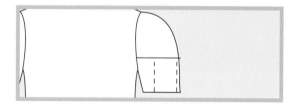

5 Form the elastic loops for the MP3 player headphone cord. Cut the elastic into two 2" pieces. On one shoulder seam (the side with the pocket for the MP3 player), open a small hole in the seam at two places with a seam ripper. Open the seam just enough to insert the ends of the elastic. Fold the elastic piece in half, matching raw ends, and insert the elastic into the sleeve opening. Stitch the seam closed, catching in the elastic ends.

Dilemma:
Don't have an MP3 player yet? Make the pocket for your cell phone instead. You can also make it to fit an MP3 player, and just use it as a cell phone holder until you get that much-wanted iPod!

Tip:

Guys: When you buy cologne, make sure that the scent goes with the soap you use in the shower. You usually don't want a sweet cologne mixed with an outdoor-scented soap. Try buying cologne in gift sets, which usually come with a body wash.

personal spaces

— Bed and Bath Décor —

You know how it is. Sometimes you have so much work to do that by the end of the week, when you finally take a minute to breathe, you realize that you have let everything in your apartment go. Your kitchen counter has a mound of dirty dishes, your bathroom has a pile of clothes on the floor, the bathtub is getting that weird ring around the edge, and the bathroom sink has dried toothpaste, make-up, hair and hairspray film all over it! The bedroom is worse. Your sheet is on top of your comforter (how does that happen anyway?), even the clean clothes are piled up in mounds, and you've started a new decorating craze — leaving half-empty water bottles all over the room. To top it off, your cell phone is ringing and you have no clue where it is!

Walking through the door of our apartment, and taking a look around, Allyce commented, "Nicole, we can't let people know we live like this!" We had two hours until we had to be ready for an eventful night with the girls, full of ice cream, cookies, pizza, movies, face masks, nail polish, candy and grilled cheese. Yes, all in that order. We girls also like to work on a project while doing all this other stuff. So while we cleaned, we brainstormed about what sewing project we might work on that evening.

"Nicole!" I heard my name called from upstairs. As I ran up the stairs, Allyce met me at the top. "I've got it! We can make a quilted blanket." Okay, I know Allyce is into sewing, and I enjoy it too, but quilting? She had lost her mind.

"All right, we're not that desperate for a project."

"No, seriously, it will be fun." I followed Allyce into her room and watched her pull out a bunch of old T-shirts from high school. "Here, we can use these as the fabric."

"No offense, hun, but I don't think that's going to make a very large blanket," I said sarcastically.

"Well you have to use some other fabric too, but this will be the main focus. We can cut the T-shirt fronts into square pieces, kind of like quilting blocks."

Yes, she'd definitely lost her mind. But to appease her, we got out some cutting rulers, needles, thread and the sewing machines. When the girls arrived, they were good sports about trying to quilt — and we had so much fun! We joked, laughed, and told stories, something we really hadn't done in a long time. Quilting definitely isn't just for grandmas.

This chapter has a few bed and bath décor projects, such as a shower curtain for an ultra-sleek new look in the bathroom, an after-shower wrap to wear around your apartment when you're getting ready, and a quilted memory blanket you'll love to make. There are also embroidery designs to coordinate with all of the projects in this chapter. So try your hand at decorating your home.

– Nicole

Avenue Montaigne

— SHOWER CURTAIN —

Supplies:

» 4 yd. print fabric (body of shower curtain)
» 2½ yd. solid cotton fabric (valance and bottom band)
» ¼ yd. white cotton fabric (machine embroidered patches)
» 5 yd. ⅜" grosgrain ribbon
» 1 pkg. wide bias tape
» Assorted machine embroidery thread
» Tear-away machine embroidery stabilizer
» Spring-type shower curtain rod
» Hanging Suit, Shoebox, Shopping Bags, Storefront and Wallet embroidery designs from the CD

Designer's Note:

Look for ways to put a different spin on an everyday product. Shower curtains are typically hung on a rod with those little hooks or rings, but you don't have to do that. Hang it through a rod pocket (like the one in this chapter), or by tabs, ribbon loops or beaded rings for a custom look.

Instructions

Cutting:

1 Cut two 60" x 45" lengths of the print fabric for the shower curtain body, and cut two 6" x 45" strips for the upper rod pocket.

2 Cut two 26" x 45" pieces from solid cotton fabric for the upper valance, and cut two 16" x 45" pieces for the bottom band.

3 Cut five 7" squares from the white cotton fabric for the machine-embroidered patches.

4 Cut six 30" lengths from the grosgrain ribbon.

5 Cut three 30" lengths from the wide bias tape.

Machine Embroidery:

1 Hoop each square of fabric with a piece of tear-away machine embroidery stabilizer. Centering each design, embroider selected embroidery motifs, following the manufacturer's directions.

2 Tear away excess stabilizer, and trim threads. Use a pair of pinking shears or a wave rotary cutter to trim each square to 6" x 6", keeping motif centered.

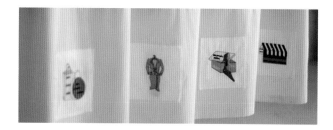

Construction:

1 Using the bottom band pieces, stitch a ½" seam, right sides together, along 16" sides. Finish seam edges, and press seam open.

2 Position each of the six embroidered squares on the panel, 5" from the top and bottom edges of the band, spacing them evenly apart. Stitch ¼" from the edge around all edges of each square, to secure the squares to the bottom band.

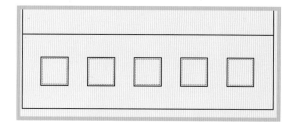

3 Place the two print fabric lengths right sides together, matching 60" sides. Stitch ½" seam, finish the edges, and press seam open.

4 Attach the bottom band to the lower edge of the print panel, matching the raw edges. Right sides together, stitch ½" seam, finish the edges, and press seam toward the shower curtain body. Hem each long edge of the shower curtain, folding under 1" twice along each long edge; press and stitch close to the hem edge. Hem the lower edge of the shower curtain, folding under 1" twice; press and stitch close to hem edge. This forms the shower curtain body.

Dilemma:
Having trouble with puckering embroidery designs? If this happens, try pressing around the edges of the design; this usually will solve your problem. If this doesn't seem to help, you may have to redo the design. If so, make sure that you use a heavier embroidery stabilizer the second time.

5 Place the two remaining solid cotton fabric upper valance pieces right sides together, matching the 26" sides. Stitch ½" seam on one 26" side, finish the edges, and press seam open. Fold under 1" twice on each short end, forming the hems; press and stitch close to the hem edge. Fold under 1" twice on the lower edge of the valance piece, forming the hem; press and stitch close to the hem edge.

6 Press open the folds on the wide bias tape. Using a piece of the bias, apply to the inside seam of the valance, overlapping the seam. Match the upper raw edge of the bias and valance, but stop the bias right above the finished hem. Stitch close to each edge of the bias, through the valance seam, and then through the center of the bias again, forming the two channels for the ribbon.

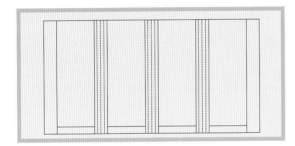

7 Create the other two channels 21" from each finished end of the valance. Apply bias and create channels as in Step 6.

8 Thread the ribbon ties through each channel, matching the raw edge of the ribbon to the upper edge of the valance. Leave the ends loose at the lower hem edge of the valance. Pin the ribbons in place along the raw edge, and then stitch close to the raw edges to hold the ribbons in place.

9 Place the valance piece on top of the shower curtain body, wrong side of the valance to the right side of the shower curtain, matching the upper raw edges. Stitch ¼" from the edges, securing the valance to the shower curtain.

10 Using the two rod pocket pieces, place 6" ends right sides together; stitch ½" seam, and press open. On each end of the long piece, turn under 1" twice, press and stitch close to the hem edge. Fold the long piece in half lengthwise, wrong sides together. Match the raw edges of this piece to the upper raw edges of the shower curtain. Stitch a ½" seam, finish the edges, and press seam toward the shower curtain body.

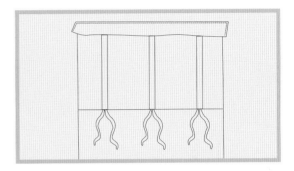

11 Place the finished shower curtain on the rod. Adjust gathers to fit the space. Pull up on the ribbons, adjusting the gathers so that the valance is at the desired height. Tie the ribbons into bows.

Tip:
Want to keep your place smelling fresh all the time but you can't use candles either because of kids, pets or clumsy friends? Try using a candle warmer. Candle warmers make it smell like you've been burning a candle for hours, and it will even help a candle last a little longer.

Classic

—COVER-UP—

Supplies:

» 1 full-size bath towel (Note: try to choose a towel that does not have a woven band on the ends)
» ⅝ yd. each of two coordinating fabrics
» 1 pkg. ¾"-wide elastic
» Iron-on hook-and-loop tape
» Thread

Designer's Note:

Recently we were in an upscale lingerie boutique looking for a cute cover-up to get from point A (the shower) to point B (the bedroom), but the only things we found cost over $100. Inspired by a designer shower wrap, we decided to create our own. Pick a theme and use it as inspiration for your wrap, choosing the same color towel or patterned fabric in those rooms. You'll have a low-cost option with a designer "spa" look.

Instructions

Cutting:

1 Hold the towel horizontally, wrap the towel around your body, and mark the side seam.

2 Measure the distance between the end of the towel and the marking, and add 1½". Cut two lower band pieces from fabric this measurement by 7" wide.

3 Measure the distance between the two side seam markings, and add 1". Cut a center back band piece from fabric this measurement by 7" wide.

4 For the upper bands, cut three pieces following the measurements above by 5" wide.

5 For the pocket, cut two 8" x 8" squares of fabric.

Construction:

1 Pin one lower band piece to the 7" edge of the center back band piece. Pin the other lower band piece to the other side of the center band to create a strip. Stitch with a ½" seam allowance, and press seam open.

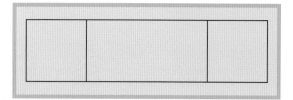

2 Turn under and press ½" along one long edge of the fabric band.

3 Pin the other long edge of the band to the lower edge of the towel (one long edge), with the right side of the band to the wrong side of the towel, and the raw edge of the band even with the edge of the towel. Match the band seams to the marked side seams. Stitch with a ½" seam allowance.

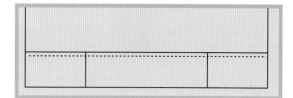

4 Press seam toward the band. Fold the band up to the right side of the towel. Pin in place, and stitch close to the top folded edge.

5 Fold the short ends of the lower band under twice, and topstitch in place.

Dilemma:
If the towel isn't quite fitting to your body, try using a longer strip of elastic. This will make your towel gather more at the top and make it fit more tightly against your body.

6 Pin the upper band pieces together along the short ends, with right sides together. Stitch with a ½" seam allowance, and press seams open.

7 Fold the band in half lengthwise, wrong sides together, and press. Open up the band, and fold each long edge to the center fold (wrong sides together); press.

8 Pin the upper band to the upper edge of the towel, with right sides together and raw edges even. Match the seams in the band to the marked side seams. Stitch along the upper and lower fold lines. Press seam toward the band.

9 Turn the short ends of the band under, and stitch in place.

10 Cut a 6" piece of elastic. Stitch the elastic to the upper edge of the towel on the inside, starting 5" from the edge. Stretch the elastic as you sew, so the upper edge gathers when the elastic is relaxed.

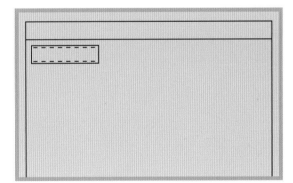

11 Wrap the towel around your body, and mark placement for the hook-and-loop tape along the top band. Following the manufacturer's directions, fuse one side of the tape to the right side of the band, and the remaining side of the tape to the wrong side of the band.

12 Pin the pocket pieces right sides together, and stitch with a ½" seam allowance along all edges, leaving an opening for turning. Turn right-side out and press. Slipstitch the opening closed.

13 Pin the pocket diagonally to the front of the towel wrap in the desired location. Stitch close to the bottom edges of the pocket.

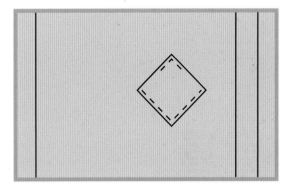

14 Stitch the top corner of the pocket in place, stitching close to the edges of the pocket.

Tip:
Does your small apartment leave you feeling a little claustrophobic? Hang mirrors on your walls. This will give the illusion that you have more open space than you really do. As an added bonus, you'll always be able to check out your style!

Time-of-Your-Life
—THROW—

Supplies:

» Selection of favorite T-shirts (11 needed)
» 2½ yd. fleece in Color 1 for blanket front pieces and strips
» 2½ yd. fleece in Color 2 for blanket front pieces and backing
» 3 yd. fusible knit interfacing
» 1 skein chenille yarn
» Tear-away embroidery stabilizer
» Machine embroidery thread, to contrast polar fleece in Color 1
» Tapestry needle
» Class of, Numbers, Freshman, Sophomore, Junior and Senior embroidery designs from the CD
» Embroidery needle

Designer's Note:

Fabric doesn't have to come from a fabric store. Look around to see what you can use, such as a T-shirt, bed sheet or fleece blanket. Some of your most creative projects can be made from unusual items.

KING

4

Junior

pride of

JAGUARS
VOLLEYBALL

Class of

Instructions

Cutting:

1 Cut 11 14" x 14" squares from fusible knit interfacing. Press interfacing onto the back side of each T-shirt, centering the imprint on the T-shirt. Cut around the interfacing square. You will need 11 T-shirt squares for this blanket. (Note: if you have designs in your T-shirts that are too small for the 14" x 14" size, cut them out after the interfacing is applied, center the design, and then stitch close to the motif edges inside a square of Color 1 fleece)

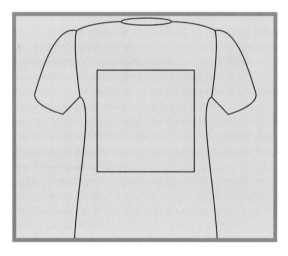

2 Cut five 14" x 14" squares from Color 1 fleece and four 14" x 14" squares from Color 2 fleece.

3 Cut six 3" x 52" strips of Color 1 fleece for piecing strips and two 3" x 75" strips of Color 1 fleece for side borders.

4 Cut one 58" x 75" piece from Color 2 fleece for the blanket backing.

Embroidery:

1 Cut a piece of tear-away stabilizer the size of the embroidery hoop, and hoop one of the Color 1 fleece squares with stabilizer for embroidery. Repeat for each embroidered motif.

2 Embroider one of the four text designs, Freshman, Sophomore, Junior and Senior, onto each fleece square.

3 Embroider "Class of" and the chosen year (i.e. graduation year) on another Color 1 fleece square.

Assembling:

1 Lay out all of the embroidered fleece squares, plain squares and T-shirt squares on a flat surface. You should have 20 total squares. Arrange the squares as you like. Lay them out 4 squares wide by 5 squares long. We used this arrangement:

T-shirt	Design	Fleece	T-shirt
T-shirt	T-shirt	T-shirt	Design
Fleece	T-shirt	Design	Fleece
Design	T-shirt	T-shirt	Design
T-shirt	T-shirt	Fleece	T-shirt

Dilemma:
Is your T-shirt collection a mishmash of different colors? Are you having trouble finding a uniformed pattern for your blanket? Try to find one color that is in all of your T-shirts. Pull that color out to use for your blanket, and it will help to coordinate all of the T-shirts together.

2 Starting with the top row of blanket squares, stitch the side seams of the squares together, right sides together, using a ½" seam allowance. Work your way across the row until all four top squares are stitched together into one long horizontal strip. Repeat the procedure for each of the remaining four rows until all five horizontal rows are assembled.

3 Using the 3" x 52" strips of fleece, stitch one strip to the lower long edge of the first row of assembled squares, with a ½" seam allowance. This acts as filler between the strips of squares. Attach another strip to the upper edge of this row. Repeat the procedure for the remaining four fleece strips until all of the fleece strips are pieced into the blanket top.

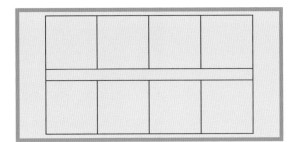

4 Stitch the 3" x 75" strips of fleece to each long side of the blanket top, right sides together, using a ½" seam allowance.

5 Lay the fleece backing on a flat surface. Place the pieced top on the backing, matching the edges as closely as possible. Pin around all of the edges, smoothing the top and bottom.

6 Place a long strand of chenille yarn in a tapestry needle. Using a running stitch, push the tapestry needle through both layers of blanket top and bottom, through center of long filler strips. Repeat until all filler strips have been stitched through. Tie the chenille yarn ends on the back side of the blanket. (Note: If your needle does not go through the fleece layers easily, use a pair of pointed embroidery scissors to poke "starter" holes as you stitch.)

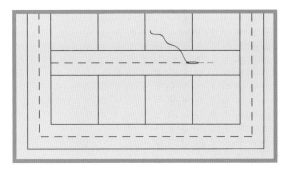

7 Trim excess fleece backing to match the blanket front edges, if necessary.

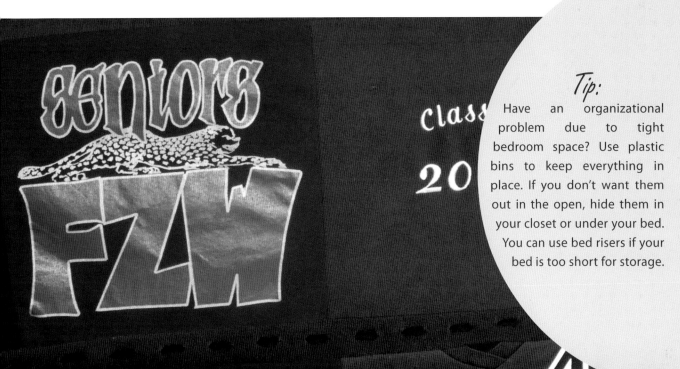

Chapter 9

diy décor
— Room and Kitchen —

It was late one Thursday night in November; Allyce was finishing up on some homework, and I was making a large pot of chili. The weather forecast was calling for snow — not much, maybe three to four inches. We knew we would have school the next day, but we were going to stay in that entire weekend and catch up on some much-needed sleep, movie watching, and anything we really wanted as long as it didn't involve much movement.

"Hey Nicole!" Allyce hollered from the living room.

"What?" I answered back.

"They are saying we might get more like six to seven inches of snow now. How much do you think we're really going to get?"

"Well, it never does what it's supposed to do, so I'm gonna say four."

"You think they'll cancel classes tomorrow?" She asked.

"I don't know. I guess it just depends on if your professors can make it into class." I told her.

As the night went on, we had finished up all our homework, studied for tests, and even had enough time to watch TV. It was a very productive night for us. Right as we were going to bed, we heard something that sounded like thunder — which was impossible since it was snowing, right? Well, sure enough, we had thunder snow. The next morning, as we got up to go to class, we realized that we were snowed in. Throughout the night we had gotten 13 inches of snow! Sure enough, school was cancelled! We decided to relax and started watching movies. Two days later, after ten movies, 12 bowls of chili (six for each of us), four games of regular Scene It, two of Disney Scene It, daily checks on MySpace, Facebook, and e-mail, it was finally official — we had cabin fever.

The roads were too bad to get out and our cars were buried under 13 inches of snow, so what were two girls to do? Since I was still a newcomer to the sewing world, Allyce wanted to make a pillow and teach me how to sew. After a few hours of sticking myself with straight pins, almost running over my finger with the sewing machine, and a fight with an unruly roll of fabric, we had an awesome pillow.

Decorating a home can be a lot of fun, especially when you have the right accessories. We decided to put a couple of things that were a little different in this chapter, such as a pillow and an unusual valance. You will be working with embroidery, so have fun and see what you can do!

– Nicole

Pillow Talk

— PILLOW —

Supplies:

» ½ yd. black-and-white cotton print
» ½ yd. sheer black organza
» 1 bag fiberfill stuffing
» Contrasting embroidery thread

Designer's Note:

When you make home-dec accessories, versatility is the operative word. Create a base project, such as a pillow, and make several accessories for it, like interchangeable decorations. You can make one for each season, every holiday, or just for a different look every day. This helps your inventive decorating become much more cents-able.

Instructions

Pillow:

1 Cut two 19" x 14" rectangles from the print fabric. Cut the sheer organza to make a 15" x 28" rectangle.

2 Place the print fabric pieces right sides together. Stitch a ½" seam around all edges, leaving a 3" opening on one side for turning and stuffing.

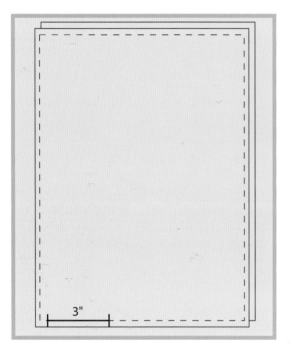

3 Clip the corners, and turn right-side out. Stuff tightly with fiberfill. Machine or hand-stitch the opening closed.

Pillow Slip:

4 Press under 1" on each long side of the sheer organza. Choose a decorative stitch on your sewing machine, and using the contrasting embroidery thread, create a line of stitching on each pressed edge of the sheer panel. If you are using small stitches, you may want to do more than one row of stitching.

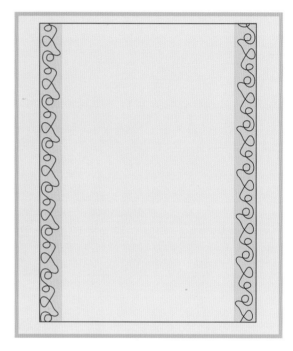

5 Place the ends of the sheer rectangle right sides together, matching the raw edges. Stitch a ½" seam. Turn the pillow slip right-side out, and slip over the pillow.

Dilemma:
What fabric should you use to make a pillow slip? For a sheer look, choose a fabric that is almost see-through, like an organza or batiste. Make sure it is a solid coordinating color so it doesn't clash with the pattern on your pillow. You can also make pillow slips from any coordinating fabric you like. Scraps can work wonders!

Tip:
Bare floors can make a room feel cold in both ambiance and temperature. If you have bare floors, find an area rug that is about two-thirds smaller than the room. This will help to warm up your place.

Girl Meets London

— VALANCE —

Currently listening to

"Maneater" by Nelly Furtado

Supplies:

- » ⅓ yd. red cotton fabric
- » ¾ yd. black fleece
- » 3 yd. print cotton fabric (for optional curtain panels)
- » 2 pairs of old blue jeans with back patch pockets
- » 4 black felt squares
- » 2 rod pocket curtain rods
- » 2½ yd. shirring tape
- » 1¼ yd. iron-on adhesive hook-and-loop tape
- » Tear-away embroidery stabilizer (optional)
- » Assorted machine embroidery threads (optional)
- » Paper-backed iron-on fusible web
- » Brit Lips, Fishnet, Phonebooth and Underground embroidery designs from the CD

Designer's Note:

Conservative looks can be shaken up a little bit. The right funky fabric and some embroidery designs can make a traditional piece of furniture young and fresh, perfect for an apartment or a loft.

Instructions

Valance: *(Note: fits windows up to 40" wide)*

1 Cut red cotton fabric to 10" x 45" and black fleece to 27" x 45".

2 Press up ½" on both long sides of the red cotton piece.

3 Cut out both back pockets from the two pairs of old jeans. Leave ½" of the blue jean all around the edges of each pocket.

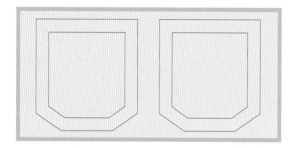

4 Folowing the embroidery machine's directions, hoop stabilizer and felt square. Embroider each of the four motifs. Tear away excess stabilizer. Cut a square of fusible web to cover back of embroidery, and fuse following directions. Repeat for each embroidery design. Cut close to embroidered edges, and then fuse one embroidery design in place on each of the four denim pockets.

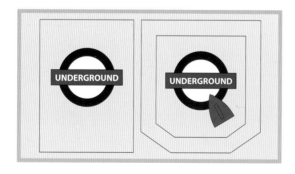

5 Press excess denim to the underside of each pocket.

6 Stitch the embellished pockets onto the red cotton fabric strip, spacing them evenly. Secure all edges of the pockets.

7 Stitch the long red strip onto the black fleece, centering the strip at top and bottom edge. Stitch close to each long edge, securing onto fleece.

8 Turn under 1" on each of the short valance ends. Stitch to secure hems.

9 Place long edges, right sides together, and stitch a ½" seam. Turn the "tube" inside out, centering the seam in the back, and red cotton strip across the front of the valance. Stitch 2" away from each long edge, forming the top and lower casings (along the edge of the red fabric panel).

10 Press the loop or soft side of the hook-and-loop tape onto the lower edge of the wrong side of the valance.

11 Place a curtain rod in the upper and lower casings to hang on the window. (Note: We secured the top curtain rod to the wall and let the bottom rod rest against the wall.)

Dilemma:
Want your embroidery designs to stand out but not take away from your fabric print? Find embroidery thread colors that coordinate well with the colors in your fabric. If you have muted colors in your pattern, don't use bright, bold colors. Make sure your colors are all in the same color palette as your print and you can be sure that they will look great together.

Curtain Panels:

1 Cut each print panel to 45" x 54". Press under each of the long side edges 1" twice, and stitch close to the hem edges. Press under the top and bottom edges 1" twice, and stitch close to hem edges. Repeat for remaining curtain panel.

2 Cut shirring tape to fit the top edge of each panel. Place shirring tape onto wrong side, matching upper edge of finished panel to edge of shirring tape. Stitch close to each long edge of the shirring tape, securing to curtain panel. Repeat for remaining curtain panel.

3 Pull up on shirring tape cords to gather each panel. Adjust as necessary to fit the valance. Tie ends of cord into a knot to hold the gathers in place.

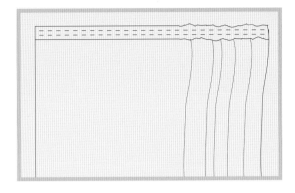

4 Press the hook side of the hook-and-loop tape onto the right side of each panel, upper edge over gathers.

5 Attach the panels to the valance, adjusting as necessary to have them hang straight.

Tip:
Decorating a kitchen when you are on a budget can be a challenge. When your money is best spent on food, it's hard to bring yourself to buy décor pieces. Try using your groceries as your décor. A bowl of whole fruit sitting on the counter, spices in a spice rack, even cookbooks can make a kitchen look pulled together and "decorative" and the best part, you can use everything you have in there.

Model Chef

— APRON —

Currently listening to

"Suzy Q" by Creedence Clearwater Revival

Supplies:

» ¾ yd. cotton print fabric
» ½ yd. solid cotton fabric
» 5 large buttons
» 2 yd. one-sided scalloped lace
» 1 ponytail holder
» Well Behaved Women embroidery design from the CD
» Tear-away embroidery stabilizer
» Thread for machine embroidery

Designer's Note:

Cute isn't always a bad thing — especially when you add a little mischief to it. A fifties apron with the right novelty-print fabric and a tongue-in-cheek embroidery design can make a cute project more modern for the working woman. Besides, when you are entertaining, you have to look the part of the competent cook — even if the nearest you usually get to gourmet is chicken fingers with barbecue sauce!

Instructions

Cutting:

1 Cut apron skirt from print fabric. Pin one end of a 20" string to the center of your fabric and tie the other end to a chalk pencil. Use this makeshift compass to draw a circle on the fabric. Repeat for the interior circle, shortening the string to 4". Cut out the interior circle.

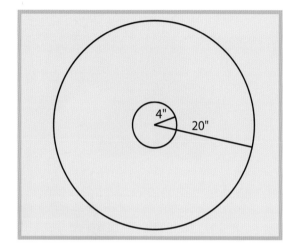

2 Cut two waist ties from print fabric, 5" x 45".

3 Cut two pieces for bib from solid fabric (see CD for pattern).

4 Cut two neck ties from print fabric, 4" x 25".

5 Cut one waistband from print fabric, 5" x 25".

6 Cut one towel loop from print fabric, 4" x 7".

Construction:

1 Finish side edges of apron skirt. Fold under ½" twice to form double hem. Topstitch close to folded edge.

2 Staystitch ⅜" away from the fabric raw edge at the top (waist). Trim fabric to staystitching before attaching apron waistband.

3 Attach the apron waistband, right sides together, to the back of the apron waist. Stitch a ½" seam. Press seam toward the waistband. Press up ½" fold on the opposite long side of the waistband.

4 Create waist ties. Fold each strip in half lengthwise, right sides together, and stitch a ½" seam on long edge and one end of the tie. Turn right-side out. Press.

5 Attach ties to each end of the waistband. Create a ½" pleat on the raw edge of each tie; pin these raw edges to the waistband side raw edges. Stitch to secure the pleats in place.

6 Finish the waistband by folding waistband wrong sides together. Stitch a ½" seam at each end, enclosing ties in seam. Stitch close to the lower edge of the waistband, encasing the seam.

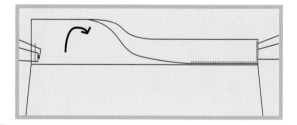

Dilemma:
Problems finding the right fabric that fits your personality? Try picking a certain theme that you particularly like. If you are into painting, try finding an artist-themed fabric. If you prefer basics, try coordinating one or two solid fabrics. The best way to find fabric is to just go shopping, either in the store or online. Follow where your eye leads you.

7. Create the apron bib. Embroider the motif on the center front piece of the solid fabric, using tear-away stabilizer and following embroidery machine instructions.

8. Place the bib pieces right sides together, and stitch a ½" seam around all sides, leaving a 3" opening at the lower edge for turning. Clip the corners and upper curves. Turn right-side out, fold in the raw edge at the opening, and press. Topstitch ¼" from the edge around all sides of the bib.

9. Attach the bib to the apron waist. Center the bib on the waistband and pin in place.

10. Create a towel loop. Fold the piece in half lengthwise, right sides together, and stitch a ½" seam. Turn the tube piece right-side out. Slide an elastic ponytail holder onto tube. Place raw ends together, stitch a ½" seam. Turn this loop over so that the seam is underneath and the elastic is at the bottom of the loop. Pin in place on waist band. Stitch buttons in place on the waist band, and stitch one button on top of the towel loop. Secure buttons in place through the bib and towel loop.

11. Create the neck ties. Fold each strip in half lengthwise and stitch a ½" seam on all sides, leaving a 3" opening for turning. Turn the ties right-sides out. Slipstitch the opening closed. Pin ties to the upper outer edges of the apron bib. Stitch buttons in place through bib and neckties.

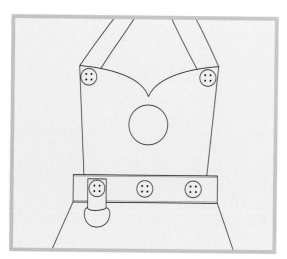

Tip:
Are you big on dishes but short on cabinets? If you need more room, use your oven as an additional storage space. You can stack pots and pans in there to keep them out of sight — just don't forget to take them out when you pre-heat the oven!

Double-Vision

— DISH TOWEL —

Supplies:

- » ½ yd. solid huck toweling fabric
- » ½ yd. cotton print fabric
- » Assorted embroidery thread
- » Tear-away embroidery stabilizer
- » Nothing Gets Me embroidery design from the CD

Designer's Note:

When embroidering a design on a terrycloth surface (like a towel), use an embroidery "topping." A topping is a sheer film that can be placed on the terry towel surface to prevent the loops of terry from getting caught in the embroidery stitches. It also makes the embroidery look smoother and neater. Most toppings tear off or dissolve in water after stitching.

NOTHING GETS ME LIKE A MAN DOING MY DISHES

Instructions

Cutting:

1 Cut one 15" x 18" piece of solid toweling fabric for the front of towel.

2 Cut one 15" x 22" piece of cotton print fabric for the back of the towel.

Construction:

1 On the toweling fabric, mark the desired placement of the embroidery design. Use the tear-away stabilizer, and embroider the motif, following the directions with your embroidery machine. Tear away the stabilizer when embroidery is complete.

2 Place the toweling and print fabric pieces right sides together, matching the short ends. Stitch a ½" seam on the short ends. You will have formed a loop of fabric.

3 Adjust the loop so that the seam is even at the top and the bottom edge, with 2" of the print fabric extending at each end. Press the seam allowances toward the solid fabric.

4 Pin long sides and stitch a ½" seam, leaving a 3" opening on one side.

5 Trim corners. Turn the towel right-side out, and tuck in raw edges; press. Topstitch close to the finished edge around all four sides of the towel.

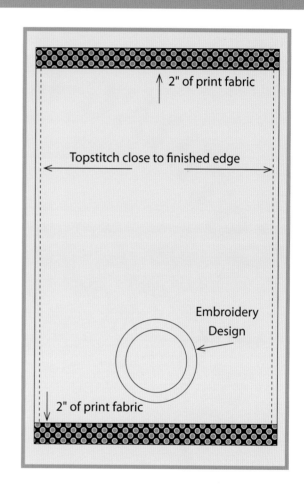

Dilemma:
Can't find a towel that coordinates with your fabric? If you can't match any of the colors in your fabric, choose from basic staple colors: black, white, cream or brown. These colors will work well and blend in with most fabrics.

NOTHING GETS ME LIKE A MAN DOING MY DISHES

Tip:

Need dishes but don't want to spend a fortune on them? Check out dollar stores to find good deals. They usually have dishes that you can mix and match. Choose different colors and pick combinations of dishes, like four green bowls, four white saucers and four blue dinner plates.

Glossary

— of Terms —

baste:

To join fabric temporarily, using large stitches that can be removed easily. You may also use basting spray.

blind hem stitch:

A stitch that looks almost invisible. It consists of one small horizontal stitch through a few fibers of the garment fabric, followed by a stitch through fibers from the hem. Make sure you don't pull the thread too much, or it could create a pucker.

bobbin:

Part of your sewing machine that contains the bottom thread (the bobbin thread) and goes into the bobbin case. Consult your sewing machine manual for more about winding and loading the bobbin.

casing:

Found on skirt or pant waists, casing refers to folding fabric to create a tube for holding elastic.

clean finish:

To turn the edge of the fabric under once and stitch a hem, after the raw edge has been serged or zig zagged. This will result in a smooth look without raveling edges.

covered button:

Buttons encased with same or like fabric as the garment or accessory.

ease:

The allowanced added to a person's body measurement when making a garment to wear. Ease allows room for movement.

embellish:

To add special stitching, appliqués, charms or other decorations to your sewing project.

fabric shears:

A sharp, accurate scissors used only for cutting fabric.

fusible interfacing:

Interfacing with a heat-activated "glue" on one side. Fusible interfacing is meant to be ironed onto fabric, usually permanently.

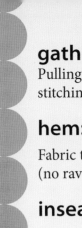

gather:

Pulling fabric together to create a "full" effect. This is done by basting two rows of stitching lines and pulling the threads together.

hem:

Fabric that is turned up on the bottom edge of a garment or sleeve for a finished edge (no raveling edges).

inseam:

Seam on the inside leg of pants that runs from the crotch to the hem.

interfacing:

Fabric used between layers of fabric to provide stabilization and form.

iron:

Tool used to straighten or press fabric and set seams. Ironing is important to ensure accurate sewing and cutting.

machine embroidery:

Decorative stitching created by using a regular sewing machine or a sewing machine designed specifically for machine embroidery.

machine needle:

Notions that come in a variety of sizes and types. There are ball-point needles used for knits, regular sharp needles for nonstretch fabrics, all-purpose needles, wing needles, wedge needles, needles of varying sizes and shapes, and twin needles for fancier stitching. Embroidery needles are meant specifically for embroidery machines.

marking chalk/pen:

Tool used to mark a cutting path along fabric.

notion:

Term for any items used for sewing other than the fabric and the machine. Notions include scissors, pins, needles, rotary cutters, etc.

pinking shears:

Scissors with a V shape along the blade edge. Pinking shears are used to cut fabric and keep it from raveling.

pins:

Used to hold patterns in place while cutting and to hold fabrics together while stitching.

pivoting:

Moving the fabric around with the machine needle in the fabric and the presser foot up.

presser foot:

The part of the sewing machine that holds the fabric in place as it is being sewn.

pucker:

When a seam gathers and causes an uneven seam appearance instead of a smooth line. During embroidery, puckering is when the fabric bunchs up around the edge of the design.

raw edge:

The edge of the fabric that has not been stitched or sewn yet.

right side:

This is the side of the fabric the print is on (or whichever side of the fabric you want for the final garment).

rotary cutter:

A pizza cutter shaped tool with an extremely sharp, round blade to cut through layers of fabric. Rotary cutters are generally straight, but they can also be pinked or have some other decorative design. Use with a rotary cutting mat.

ruler:

A clear, straight-edged plastic tool with markings every ¼" used for measuring. Use 6"-wide rulers for guiding a rotary cutter.

running stitch:

A simple stitch made by running the thread over and under the fabric.

satin stitch:

A zigzag stitch with a shortened stitch length to create parallel stitches.

seam:

A line of stitching that holds two pieces of fabric together.

seam allowance:

The amount of fabric between the seam stitching and the cut edge. For clothing, ⅝" seam allowances are common. In this book, we've used ½" seam allowances for home décor and ⅝" for clothing.

selvage:

The edge of the fabric which is unable to fray; usually, the selvage is where the fabric information is.

serger:

A type of sewing machine that cuts and finishes the seam allowance in one step. Sergers use multiple spools of thread and sew much more quickly than a regular sewing machine.

shank button:

A flat-faced button with a loop of plastic or metal on the back for attaching it to a garment.

stabilizer:

Woven or non-woven fabric used to support embroidery stitches. Stabilizer is placed underneath the fabric to keep the embroidery from puckering.

stay-stitching:

Stitching done inside the seam allowance, before construction, to stabilize curved or slanted edges. Stay-stitching is also used to attach interfacing.

straight stitch:

Basic stitch that most sewing machines make. Straight stitches are used for most garment construction.

tack:

A stitch used to hold a piece of fabric in place.

tape measure:

Flexible measuring device, usually made of cloth, with inch marks and centimeters on both sides. Tape measures are especially important for measuring fit for garments.

thread:

A complimentary or like color is chosen to construct projects or garments. Embroidery thread is especially for embroidering designs and should not be used in project or garment construction.

topstitching:

Stitching that shows on the outside of the garment.

trim:

The finishing touch on a project. Trims include ribbon, lace, cording and piping.

wrong side:

The side of the fabric that will not show in the final project.

zigzag stitch:

A stitch that goes from one side to the other. Zigzag stitches are frequently used as a finishing stitch or to prevent raveling.

Embroidery

— Design Index —

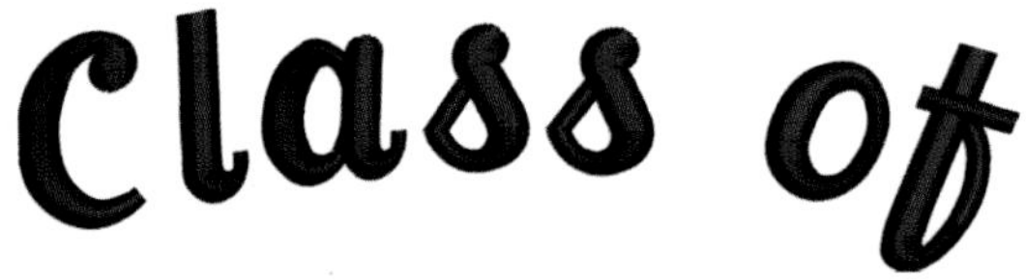

Class of
class of

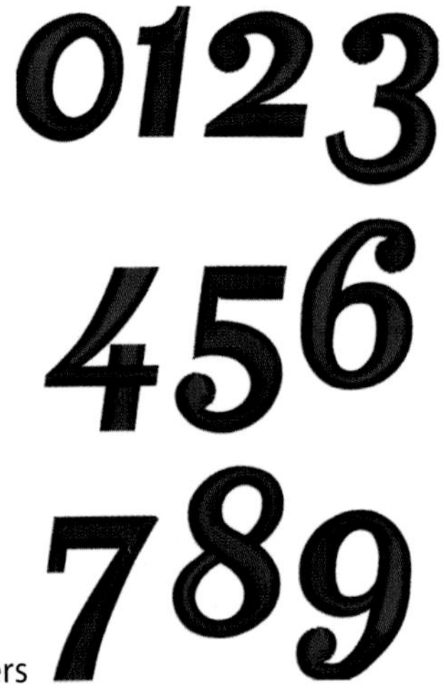

0123
456
789

numbers

A B C D E F
G H I J K L
M N O P Q
R S T U V
W X Y Z

monogram lettering

Freshman
freshman

Sophomore
sophomore

Junior
junior

Senior
senior

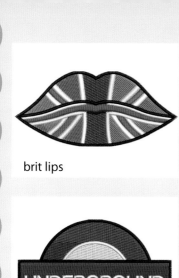
brit lips

underground

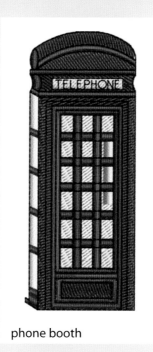
phone booth

well behaved women

nothing gets me

hanging suit

shopping bags

compass

storefront

wallet

fishnet

shoebox

Resources

American & Efird
www.amefird.com
Consumer.Homepage@amefird.com
1-800-453-5128
Thread and trims

Bernina
www.berninausa.com
1-630-978-2500
Sewing machines and accessories

Clover
www.clover-usa.com
cni@clover-usa.com
Sewing, knitting and embroidery tools

Duncan Crafts
www.duncancrafts.com
1-800-438-6226
Glues, embellishments, paints and dyes

Fiskars
www.fiskars.com
socconsumeraffairs@fiskars.com
1-866-348-5661
Craft tools

Gingher
www.gingher.com
singerherinfo@gingher.com
1-800-446-4437
Scissors and shears

Kandi Corp
www.kandicorp.com
1-800-985-2634
Hot-fix crystals and applicators

Michael Miller Fabrics
www.michaelmillerfabrics.com
info@michaelmillerfabrics.com
212-704-0774
Fashion fabrics

O'lipfa
www.olipfa.com
info@olipfa.com
1-866-861-1424
Acrylic rulers and measuring tools

Prym Dritz
www.dritz.com
Sewing, quilting and crafting notions

Robert Kaufman Fabrics
www.robertkaufman.com
info@robertkaufman.com
1-800-877-2066
Fashion fabrics

Velco
www.velcro.com
Hook-and-loop tape

Wrights
www.wrights.com
help@wrights.com
1-877-597-4448
Bias tapes, sewing tools and notions

Nicole Thieret

Nicole is an accomplished student at Stephens College in Columbia, MO, where she is majoring in marketing, public relations and advertising with a minor in special events planning. Currently, Nicole serves advertising agency Woodruff Sweitzer as project manager for the Roots 'N Blues 'N BBQ festival. A former dance champion, her many passions include jazz and lyrical dance, fashion forecasting, writing and volunteer work in the community. Nicole continues to write and work as an event coordinator.

Allyce King

Allyce King is a student at Stephens College in Columbia, MO. She is majoring in fashion design with a minor in marketing. She has been sewing, designing and making unique things since the age of six. Her first love is Paddy, a Yorkie who lives with her at college. She enjoys sewing, designing, painting, drawing, scrapbooking and running with her dog in her free time. Allyce writes for sewing and embroidery magazines and continuously comes up with more creative ideas than she can bring to completion. Watch for Allyce on the new sewing video podcast, *DIY Style*.